Practice the COMPASS®!

COMPASS® Practice Test Questions

Checked for writing	Staff Initials	Date
✓	Cnw	5-27-14
✓	old	8/16/14
✓	ML	8-8-16
✓	ferr	8/25/16
✓	cmp	11-9-18

Published by

Complete **TEST** **Preparation Inc.**

We strongly recommend that students check with exam providers for up-to-date information regarding test content.

ISBN-13: 978-1928077060 (Complete Test Preparation Inc.)

ISBN-10: 1928077064

Published by
Complete Test Preparation Inc.
921 Foul Bay Rd.
Victoria BC Canada V8S 4H9
Visit us on the web at http://www.test-preparation.ca
Printed in the USA

About Complete Test Preparation

The Complete Test Preparation Team has been publishing high quality study materials since 2005. Thousands of students visit our websites every year, and thousands of students, teachers and parents all over the world have purchased our teaching materials, curriculum, study guides and practice tests.

Complete Test Preparation is committed to providing students with the best study materials and practice tests available on the market. Members of our team combine years of teaching experience, with experienced writers and editors, all with advanced degrees.

Team Members for this publication

Editor: Brian Stocker MA
Contributor: Dr. C. Gregory
Contributor: Dr. G. A. Stocker DDS
Contributor: D. A. Stocker M. Ed.
Contributor: Sheila M. Hynes, MES York, BA (Hons)
Contributor: Elizabeta Petrovic MSc (Mathematics)
Contributor: Kelley O'Malley BA (English)

Feedback

We welcome your feedback. Email us at feedback@test-preparation.ca with your comments and suggestions. We carefully review all suggestions and often incorporate reader suggestions into upcoming versions. As a Print on Demand Publisher, we update our products frequently.

 Find us on Facebook

www.facebook.com/CompleteTestPreparation

The Environment and Sustainability

Environmental consciousness is important for the continued growth of our company. In addition to eco-balancing each title, as a print on demand publisher, we only print units as orders come in, which greatly reduces excess printing and waste. This revolutionary printing technology also eliminates carbon emissions from trucks hauling boxes of books everywhere to warehouses. We also maintain a commitment to recycling any waste materials that may result from the printing process. We continue to review our manufacturing practices on an ongoing basis to ensure we are doing our part to protect and improve the environment.

Contents

Getting Started

CONGRATULATIONS! By deciding to take the COMPASS® Exam, you have taken the first step toward a great future! Of course, there is no point in taking this important examination unless you intend to do your very best in order to earn the highest grade you possibly can. That means getting yourself organized and discovering the best approaches, methods and strategies to master the material. Yes, that will require real effort and dedication on your part but if you are willing to focus your energy and devote the study time necessary, before you know it you will be on you will be opening that letter of acceptance to the school of your dreams!

We know that taking on a new endeavour can be a little scary, and it is easy to feel unsure of where to begin. That's where we come in. This study guide is designed to help you improve your test-taking skills, show you a few tricks of the trade and increase both your competency and confidence.

The COMPASS Exam

The COMPASS® exam is composed of four main sections, reading, mathematics, sentence skills and writing. The reading section consists of reading comprehension questions. The mathematics section contains, arithmetic, algebra, college level math, geometry and trigonometry. The sentence skills section contains questions on sentence structure and rewriting sentences. The writing section contains an essay question.

The COMPASS exam is computer based and adaptive. This means if you answer a questions correctly, the next question will be more difficulty until you reach your level of difficulty. If you answer incorrectly and you are not already at the lowest level of difficulty, the next question will be easier. Each question is multiple-choice, and the exact number of questions varies from student to student depending upon how skilled the student is in a particular area.

While we seek to make our guide as comprehensive as possible, it is important to note that like all exams, the COMPASS® Exam might be adjusted at some future point. New material might be added, or content that is no longer relevant or applicable might be removed. It is always a good idea to give the materials you receive when you register to take the COMPASS® a careful review.

The COMPASS® Study Plan

Now that you have made the decision to take the COMPASS®, it is time to get started. Before you do another thing, you will need to figure out a plan of attack. The very best study tip is to start early! The longer the time period you devote to regular study practice, the more likely you will be to retain the material and be able to access it quickly. If you thought that 1x20 is the same as 2x10, guess what? It really is not, when it comes to study time. Reviewing material for just an hour per day over the course of 20 days is far better than studying for two hours a day for only 10 days. The more often you revisit a particular piece of information, the better you will know it. Not only will your grasp and understanding be better, but your ability to reach into your brain and quickly and efficiently pull out the tidbit you need, will be greatly enhanced as well.

The great Chinese scholar and philosopher Confucius believed that true knowledge could be defined as knowing both what you know and what you do not know. The first step in preparing for the COMPASS® is to assess your strengths and weaknesses. You may already have an idea of what you know and what you do not know, but evaluating yourself using our Self- Assessment modules for each of the three areas, Math, Writing and Reading Comprehension, will clarify the details.

Making a Study Schedule

In order to make your study time most productive you will
need to develop a study plan. The purpose of the plan is to
organize all the bits of pieces of information in such a way
that you will not feel overwhelmed. Rome was not built in a
day, and learning everything you will need to know in order
to pass the COMPASS® is going to take time, too. Arranging
the material you need to learn into manageable chunks is
the best way to go. Each study session should make you feel
as though you have succeeded in accomplishing your goal,
and your goal is simply to learn what you planned to learn
during that particular session. Try to organize the content
in such a way that each study session builds upon previous
ones. That way, you will retain the information, be better
able to access it, and review the previous bits and pieces at
the same time.

Self-assessment

The Best Study Tip! The very best study tip is to start early!
The longer you study regularly, the more you will retain and
'learn' the material. Studying for 1 hour per day for 20 days
is far better than studying for 2 hours for 10 days.

What don't you know?

The first step is to assess your strengths and weaknesses.
You may already have an idea of where your weaknesses are,
or you can take our Self-assessment modules for each of the
areas, Reading Comprehension, Arithmetic, Essay Writing,
Algebra and College Level Math.

Exam Component	Rate 1 to 5
Reading Comprehension	
Making Inferences	

Main idea	
Arithmetic	
Decimals Percent and Fractions	
Problem solving (Word Problems)	
Basic Algebra	
Simple Geometry	
Problem Solving	
Essay Writing	
Sentence Skills	
Sentence Correction	
Basic English Grammar and Usage	
Algebra	
Exponents	
Linear Equations	
Quadratics	
Polynomials	
College Level	
Coordinate Geometry	
Trigonometry	
Polynomials	
Logarithms	
Sequences	

Making a Study Schedule

The key to making a study plan is to divide the material you need to learn into manageable size and learn it, while at the same time reviewing the material that you already know.

Using the table above, any scores of three or below, you need to spend time learning, going over and practicing this subject area. A score of four means you need to review the material, but you don't have to spend time re-learning. A score of five and you are OK with just an occasional review before the exam.

A score of zero or one means you really do need to work on this and you should allocate the most time and give it the highest priority. Some students prefer a 5-day plan and others a 10-day plan. It also depends on how much time you have until the exam.

Here is an example of a 5-day plan based on an example from the table above:

Main Idea: 1 Study 1 hour everyday – review on last day
Fractions: 3 Study 1 hour for 2 days then ½ hour and then review
Algebra: 4 Review every second day
Grammar & Usage: 2 Study 1 hour on the first day – then ½ hour everyday
Reading Comprehension: 5 Review for ½ hour every other day
Geometry: 5 Review for ½ hour every other day

Using this example, geometry and reading comprehension are good and only need occasional review. Algebra is good and needs 'some' review. Fractions need a bit of work, grammar and usage needs a lot of work and Main Idea is very weak and need the majority of time. Based on this, here is a sample study plan:

Day	Subject	Time
Monday		
Study	Main Idea	1 hour
Study	Grammar & Usage	1 hour
	½ hour break	
Study	Fractions	1 hour
Review	Algebra	½ hour

Tuesday		
Study	Main Idea	1 hour
Study	Grammar & Usage	½ hour
	½ hour break	
Study	Fractions	½ hour
Review	Algebra	½ hour
Review	Geometry	½ hour
Wednesday		
Study	Main Idea	1 hour
Study	Grammar & Usage	½ hour
	½ hour break	
Study	Fractions	½ hour
Review	Geometry	½ hour
Thursday		
Study	Main Idea	½ hour
Study	Grammar & Usage	½ hour
Review	Fractions	½ hour
	½ hour break	
Review	Geometry	½ hour
Review	Algebra	½ hour
Friday		
Review	Main Idea	½ hour
Review	Grammar & Usage	½ hour
Review	Fractions	½ hour
	½ hour break	
Review	Algebra	½ hour
Review	Grammar & Usage	½ hour

Using this example, adapt the study plan to your own schedule. This schedule assumes 2 ½ - 3 hours available to study everyday for a 5 day period.

First, write out what you need to study and how much. Next figure out how many days you have before the test. Note, do NOT study on the last day before the test. On the last day before the test, you won't learn anything and will probably only confuse yourself.

Make a table with the days before the test and the number of hours you have available to study each day. We suggest working with 1 hour and ½ hour time slots.

Start filling in the blanks, with the subjects you need to study the most getting the most time and the most regular time slots (i.e. everyday) and the subjects that you know getting the least time (e.g. ½ hour every other day, or every 3rd day).

Tips for making a schedule

Once you make a schedule, stick with it! Make your study sessions reasonable. If you make a study schedule and don't stick with it, you set yourself up for failure. Instead, schedule study sessions that are a bit shorter and set yourself up for success! Make sure your study sessions are do-able. Studying is hard work but after you pass, you can party and take a break!

Schedule breaks. Breaks are just as important as study time. Work out a rotation of studying and breaks that works for you.

Build up study time. If you find it hard to sit still and study for 1 hour straight through, build up to it. Start with 20 minutes, and then take a break. Once you get used to 20-minute study sessions, increase the time to 30 minutes. Gradually work you way up to 1 hour.

40 minutes to 1 hour are optimal. Studying for longer than this is tiring and not productive. Studying for shorter isn't long enough to be productive.

Studying Math. Studying Math is different from studying other subjects because you use a different part of your brain. The best way to study math is to practice everyday. This will train your mind to think in a mathematical way. If you miss a day or days, the mathematical mind-set is gone and you have to start all over again to build it up.

Study and practice math everyday for at least 5 days before the exam.

Practice Test Questions Set 1

The questions below are not exactly the same as you will find on the COMPASS® - that would be too easy! And nobody knows what the questions will be and they change all the time. Below are general questions that cover the same subject areas as the COMPASS®. So while the format and exact wording of the questions may differ slightly, and change from year to year, if you can answer the questions below, you will have no problem with the COMPASS®.

For the best results, take these practice test questions as if it were the real exam. Set aside time when you will not be disturbed, and a location that is quiet and free of distractions. Read the instructions carefully, read each question carefully, and answer to the best of your ability.
Use the bubble answer sheets provided. When you have completed the practice questions, check your answer against the Answer Key and read the explanation provided.

Do not attempt more than one set of practice test questions in one day. After completing the first practice test, wait two or three days before attempting the second set of questions.

Reading Answer Sheet

1. Ⓐ Ⓑ Ⓒ Ⓓ   11. Ⓐ Ⓑ Ⓒ Ⓓ   21. Ⓐ Ⓑ Ⓒ Ⓓ

2. Ⓐ Ⓑ Ⓒ Ⓓ   12. Ⓐ Ⓑ Ⓒ Ⓓ   22. Ⓐ Ⓑ Ⓒ Ⓓ

3. Ⓐ Ⓑ Ⓒ Ⓓ   13. Ⓐ Ⓑ Ⓒ Ⓓ   23. Ⓐ Ⓑ Ⓒ Ⓓ

4. Ⓐ Ⓑ Ⓒ Ⓓ   14. Ⓐ Ⓑ Ⓒ Ⓓ   24. Ⓐ Ⓑ Ⓒ Ⓓ

5. Ⓐ Ⓑ Ⓒ Ⓓ   15. Ⓐ Ⓑ Ⓒ Ⓓ   25. Ⓐ Ⓑ Ⓒ Ⓓ

6. Ⓐ Ⓑ Ⓒ Ⓓ   16. Ⓐ Ⓑ Ⓒ Ⓓ   26. Ⓐ Ⓑ Ⓒ Ⓓ

7. Ⓐ Ⓑ Ⓒ Ⓓ   17. Ⓐ Ⓑ Ⓒ Ⓓ   27. Ⓐ Ⓑ Ⓒ Ⓓ

8. Ⓐ Ⓑ Ⓒ Ⓓ   18. Ⓐ Ⓑ Ⓒ Ⓓ   28. Ⓐ Ⓑ Ⓒ Ⓓ

9. Ⓐ Ⓑ Ⓒ Ⓓ   19. Ⓐ Ⓑ Ⓒ Ⓓ   29. Ⓐ Ⓑ Ⓒ Ⓓ

10. Ⓐ Ⓑ Ⓒ Ⓓ   20. Ⓐ Ⓑ Ⓒ Ⓓ   30. Ⓐ Ⓑ Ⓒ Ⓓ

Mathematics Answer Sheet

1. (A) (B) (C) (D)   21. (A) (B) (C) (D)   41. (A) (B) (C) (D)

2. (A) (B) (C) (D)   22. (A) (B) (C) (D)   42. (A) (B) (C) (D)

3. (A) (B) (C) (D)   23. (A) (B) (C) (D)   43. (A) (B) (C) (D)

4. (A) (B) (C) (D)   24. (A) (B) (C) (D)   44. (A) (B) (C) (D)

5. (A) (B) (C) (D)   25. (A) (B) (C) (D)   45. (A) (B) (C) (D)

6. (A) (B) (C) (D)   26. (A) (B) (C) (D)   46. (A) (B) (C) (D)

7. (A) (B) (C) (D)   27. (A) (B) (C) (D)   47. (A) (B) (C) (D)

8. (A) (B) (C) (D)   28. (A) (B) (C) (D)   48. (A) (B) (C) (D)

9. (A) (B) (C) (D)   29. (A) (B) (C) (D)   49. (A) (B) (C) (D)

10. (A) (B) (C) (D)   30. (A) (B) (C) (D)   50. (A) (B) (C) (D)

11. (A) (B) (C) (D)   31. (A) (B) (C) (D)   51. (A) (B) (C) (D)

12. (A) (B) (C) (D)   32. (A) (B) (C) (D)   52. (A) (B) (C) (D)

13. (A) (B) (C) (D)   33. (A) (B) (C) (D)   53. (A) (B) (C) (D)

14. (A) (B) (C) (D)   34. (A) (B) (C) (D)   54. (A) (B) (C) (D)

15. (A) (B) (C) (D)   35. (A) (B) (C) (D)   55. (A) (B) (C) (D)

16. (A) (B) (C) (D)   36. (A) (B) (C) (D)   56. (A) (B) (C) (D)

17. (A) (B) (C) (D)   37. (A) (B) (C) (D)   57. (A) (B) (C) (D)

18. (A) (B) (C) (D)   38. (A) (B) (C) (D)   58. (A) (B) (C) (D)

19. (A) (B) (C) (D)   39. (A) (B) (C) (D)   59. (A) (B) (C) (D)

20. (A) (B) (C) (D)   40. (A) (B) (C) (D)   60. (A) (B) (C) (D)

Sentence Skills Answer Sheet

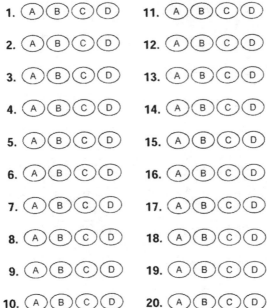

1. Ⓐ Ⓑ Ⓒ Ⓓ   11. Ⓐ Ⓑ Ⓒ Ⓓ

2. Ⓐ Ⓑ Ⓒ Ⓓ   12. Ⓐ Ⓑ Ⓒ Ⓓ

3. Ⓐ Ⓑ Ⓒ Ⓓ   13. Ⓐ Ⓑ Ⓒ Ⓓ

4. Ⓐ Ⓑ Ⓒ Ⓓ   14. Ⓐ Ⓑ Ⓒ Ⓓ

5. Ⓐ Ⓑ Ⓒ Ⓓ   15. Ⓐ Ⓑ Ⓒ Ⓓ

6. Ⓐ Ⓑ Ⓒ Ⓓ   16. Ⓐ Ⓑ Ⓒ Ⓓ

7. Ⓐ Ⓑ Ⓒ Ⓓ   17. Ⓐ Ⓑ Ⓒ Ⓓ

8. Ⓐ Ⓑ Ⓒ Ⓓ   18. Ⓐ Ⓑ Ⓒ Ⓓ

9. Ⓐ Ⓑ Ⓒ Ⓓ   19. Ⓐ Ⓑ Ⓒ Ⓓ

10. Ⓐ Ⓑ Ⓒ Ⓓ   20. Ⓐ Ⓑ Ⓒ Ⓓ

Part 1 - Reading

Questions 1 – 4 refer to the following passage.

Infectious Diseases

An infectious disease is a clinically evident illness resulting from the presence of pathogenic agents, such as viruses, bacteria, fungi, protozoa, multi-cellular parasites, and unusual proteins known as prions. Infectious pathologies are also called communicable diseases or transmissible diseases, due to their potential of transmission from one person or species to another by a replicating agent (as opposed to a toxin).

Transmission of an infectious disease can occur in many different ways. Physical contact, liquids, food, body fluids, contaminated objects, and airborne inhalation can all transmit infecting agents.

Transmissible diseases that occur through contact with an ill person, or objects touched by them, are especially infective, and are sometimes referred to as contagious diseases. Communicable diseases that require a more specialized route of infection, such as through blood or needle transmission, or sexual transmission, are usually not regarded as contagious.

The term infectivity describes the ability of an organism to enter, survive and multiply in the host, while the infectiousness of a disease indicates the comparative ease with which the disease is transmitted. An infection however, is not synonymous with an infectious disease, as an infection may not cause important clinical symptoms. [3]

1. What can we infer from the first paragraph in this passage?

   a. Sickness from a toxin can be easily transmitted from one person to another.

   b. Sickness from an infectious disease can be easily transmitted from one person to another.

   c. Few sicknesses are transmitted from one person to another.

   d. Infectious diseases are easily treated.

2. What are two other names for infections' pathologies?

   a. Communicable diseases or transmissible diseases

   b. Communicable diseases or terminal diseases

   c. Transmissible diseases or preventable diseases

   d. Communicative diseases or unstable diseases

3. What does infectivity describe?

   a. The inability of an organism to multiply in the host.

   b. The inability of an organism to reproduce.

   c. The ability of an organism to enter, survive and multiply in the host.

   d. The ability of an organism to reproduce in the host.

4. How do we know an infection is not synonymous with an infectious disease?

   a. Because an infectious disease destroys infections with enough time.

   b. Because an infection may not cause clinical symptoms or impair host function.

   c. We do not. The two are synonymous.

   d. Because an infection is too fatal to be an infectious disease.

Questions 5 – 7 refer to the following passage.

Thunderstorms

The first stage of a thunderstorm is the cumulus stage, or developing stage. In this stage, masses of moisture are lifted upwards into the atmosphere. The trigger for this lift can be insulation heating the ground producing thermals, areas where two winds converge, forcing air upwards, or where winds blow over terrain of increasing elevation. Moisture in the air rapidly cools into liquid drops of water, which appears as cumulus clouds.

As the water vapor condenses into liquid, latent heat is released which warms the air, causing it to become less dense than the surrounding dry air. The warm air rises in an updraft through the process of convection (hence the term convective precipitation). This creates a low-pressure zone beneath the forming thunderstorm. In a typical thunderstorm, approximately 5×10^8 kg of water vapor is lifted, and the amount of energy released when this condenses is about equal to the energy used by a city of 100,000 in a month. [4]

5. The cumulus stage of a thunderstorm is the

    a. The last stage of the storm.

    b. The middle stage of the storm formation.

    c. The beginning of the thunderstorm.

    d. The period after the thunderstorm has ended.

6. One of the ways the air is warmed is

    a. Air moving downwards, which creates a high-pressure zone.

    b. Air cooling and becoming less dense, causing it to rise.

    c. Moisture moving downward toward the earth.

    d. Heat created by water vapor condensing into liquid.

7. Identify the correct sequence of events.

a. Warm air rises, water droplets condense, creating more heat, and the air rises further.

b. Warm air rises and cools, water droplets condense, causing low pressure.

c. Warm air rises and collects water vapor, the water vapor condenses as the air rises, which creates heat, and causes the air to rise further.

d. None of the above.

Questions 8 – 10 refer to the following passage.

The US Weather Service

The United States National Weather Service classifies thunderstorms as severe when they reach a predetermined level. Usually, this means the storm is strong enough to inflict wind or hail damage. In most of the United States, a storm is considered severe if winds reach over 50 knots (58 mph or 93 km/h), hail is ¾ inch (2 cm) diameter or larger, or if meteorologists report funnel clouds or tornadoes. In the Central Region of the United States National Weather Service, the hail threshold for a severe thunderstorm is 1 inch (2.5 cm) in diameter. Though a funnel cloud or tornado indicates the presence of a severe thunderstorm, the various meteorological agencies would issue a tornado warning rather than a severe thunderstorm warning in this case.

Meteorologists in Canada define a severe thunderstorm as either having tornadoes, wind gusts of 90 km/h or greater, hail 2 centimeters in diameter or greater, rainfall more than 50 millimeters in 1 hour, or 75 millimeters in 3 hours.

Severe thunderstorms can develop from any type of thunderstorm. [5]

8. What is the purpose of this passage?

a. Explaining when a thunderstorm turns into a tornado.

b. Explaining who issues storm warnings, and when these warnings should be issued.

c. Explaining when meteorologists consider a thunderstorm severe.

d. None of the above.

9. It is possible to infer from this passage that

a. Different areas and countries have different criteria for determining a severe storm.

b. Thunderstorms can include lightning and tornadoes, as well as violent winds and large hail.

c. If someone spots both a thunderstorm and a tornado, meteorological agencies will immediately issue a severe storm warning.

d. Canada has a much different alert system for severe storms, with criteria that are far less.

10. What would the Central Region of the United States National Weather Service do if hail was 2.7 cm in diameter?

a. Not issue a severe thunderstorm warning.

b. Issue a tornado warning.

c. Issue a severe thunderstorm warning.

d. Sleet must also accompany the hail before the Weather Service will issue a storm warning.

Questions 11 – 13 refer to the following passage.

Clouds

A cloud is a visible mass of droplets or frozen crystals floating in the atmosphere above the surface of the Earth or
other planetary bodies. Another type of cloud is a mass of
material in space, attracted by gravity, called interstellar
clouds and nebulae. The branch of meteorology which stud-
ies clouds is called nephrology. When we are speaking of
Earth clouds, water vapor is usually the condensing sub-
stance, which forms small droplets or ice crystal. These crystals are typically 0.01 mm in diameter. Dense, deep clouds
reflect most light, so they appear white, at least from the top.
Cloud droplets scatter light very efficiently, so the further
into a cloud light travels, the weaker it gets. This accounts
for the gray or dark appearance at the base of large clouds.
Thin clouds may appear to have acquired the color of their
environment or background. [6]

11. What are clouds made of?

    a. Water droplets

    b. Ice crystals

    c. Ice crystals and water droplets

    d. Clouds on Earth are made of ice crystals and water
droplets

12. The main idea of this passage is

    a. Condensation occurs in clouds, having an intense
effect on the weather on the surface of the earth.

    b. Atmospheric gases are responsible for the gray color
of clouds just before a severe storm happens.

    c. A cloud is a visible mass of droplets or frozen crys-
tals floating in the atmosphere above the surface of the
Earth or other planetary body.

    d. Clouds reflect light in varying amounts and degrees,
depending on the size and concentration of the water
droplets.

13. Why are clouds white on top and grey on the bottom?

a. Because water droplets inside the cloud do not reflect light, it appears white, and the further into the cloud the light travels, the less light is reflected making the bottom appear dark.

b. Because water droplets outside the cloud reflect light, it appears dark, and the further into the cloud the light travels, the more light is reflected making the bottom appear white.

c. Because water droplets inside the cloud reflects light, making it appear white, and the further into the cloud the light travels, the more light is reflected making the bottom appear dark.

d. None of the above.

Questions 14 - 17 refer to the following passage.

Keeping Tropical Fish

Keeping tropical fishes at home or in your office used to be very popular. Today interest has declined, but it remains as rewarding and relaxing a hobby as ever. Ask any tropical fish hobbyist, and you will hear how soothing and relaxing watching colorful fish live their lives in the aquarium. If you are considering keeping tropical fish as pets, here is a list of the basic equipment you will need.

A filter is essential for keeping your aquarium clean and your fish alive and healthy. There are different types and sizes of filters and the right size for you depends on the size of the aquarium and the level of stocking. Generally, you need a filter with a 3 to 5 times turn over rate per hour. This means that the water in the tank should go through the filter about 3 to 5 times per hour.

Most tropical fish do well in water temperatures ranging between 24°C and 26°C, though each has its own ideal water temperature. A heater with a thermostat is necessary to regulate the water temperature. Some heaters are submersible and others are not, so check carefully before you buy.

Lights are also necessary, and come in a large variety of types, strengths and sizes. A light source is necessary for plants in the tank to photosynthesize and give the tank a more attractive appearance. Even if you plan on using plastic plants, the fish still require light, although in this case you can use a lower strength light source.

A hood is necessary to keep dust, dirt and unwanted materials out of the tank. In some cases the hood can also help prevent evaporation. Another requirement is aquarium gravel. This will help improve the aesthetics of the aquarium and is necessary if you plan on having real plants.

14. What is the general tone of this article?

    a. Formal

    b. Informal

    c. Technical

    d. Opinion

15. Which of the following can not be inferred?

    a. Gravel is good for aquarium plants.

    b. Fewer people have aquariums in their office than at home.

    c. The larger the tank, the larger the filter required.

    d. None of the above.

16. What evidence does the author provide to support their claim that aquarium lights are necessary?

    a. Plants require light.

    b. Fish and plants require light.

    c. The author does not provide evidence for this statement.

    d. Aquarium lights make the aquarium more attractive.

17. Which of the following is an opinion?

    a. Filter with a 3 to 5 times turn over rate per hour are required.

    b. Aquarium gravel improves the aesthetics of the aquarium.

    c. An aquarium hood keeps dust, dirt and unwanted materials out of the tank.

    d. Each type of tropical fish has its own ideal water temperature.

Questions 18 - 20 refer to the following passage.

Ways Characters Communicate in Theater

Playwrights give their characters voices in a way that gives depth and added meaning to what happens on stage during their play. There are different types of speech in scripts that allow characters to talk with themselves, with other characters, and even with the audience.

It is very unique to theater that characters may talk "to themselves." When characters do this, the speech they give is called a soliloquy. Soliloquies are usually poetic, introspective, moving, and can tell audience members about the feelings, motivations, or suspicions of an individual character without that character having to reveal them to other characters on stage. "To be or not to be" is a famous soliloquy given by Hamlet as he considers difficult but important themes, such as life and death.

The most common type of communication in plays is when one character is speaking to another or a group of other characters. This is generally called dialogue, but can also be called monologue if one character speaks without being interrupted for a long time. It is not necessarily the most important type of communication, but it is the most common because the plot of the play cannot really progress without it.

Lastly, and most unique to theater (although it has been used somewhat in film) is when a character speaks directly to the audience. This is called an aside, and scripts usually specifically direct actors to do this. Asides are usually comical, an inside joke between the character and the audience, and very short. The actor will usually face the audience when delivering them, even if it's for a moment, so the audience can recognize this move as an aside.

All three of these types of communication are important to the art of theater, and have been perfected by famous playwrights like Shakespeare. Understanding these types of communication can help an audience member grasp what is artful about the script and action of a play.

18. According to the passage, characters in plays communicate to

    a. move the plot forward

    b. show the private thoughts and feelings of one character

    c. make the audience laugh

    d. add beauty and artistry to the play

19. When Hamlet delivers "To be or not to be", he can most likely be described as

    a. solitary

    b. thoughtful

    c. dramatic

    d. hopeless

20. It can be understood that by the phrase "give their characters voices," the author means that

    a. playwrights are generous

    b. playwrights are changing the sound or meaning of characters' voices to fit what they had in mind

    c. dialogue is important in creating characters

    d. playwrights may be the parent of one of their actors and literally give them their voice

20. The author uses parentheses to punctuate "although it has been used somewhat in film"

    a. to show that films are less important

    b. instead of using commas so that the sentence is not interrupted

    c. because parenthesis help separate details that are not as important

    d. to show that films are not as artistic

Mathematics

1. Brad has agreed to buy everyone a Coke. Each drink costs $1.89, and there are 5 friends. Estimate Brad's cost.

   a. $7
   b. $8
   c. $10
   d. $12

2. Sarah weighs 25 pounds more than Tony does. If together they weigh 205 pounds, how much does Sarah weigh approximately in kilograms? Assume 1 pound = 0.4535 kilograms.

   a. 41
   b. 48
   c. 50
   d. 52

3. What fraction of $1500 is $75?

   a. 1/14
   b. 3/5
   c. 7/10
   d. 1/20

4. Estimate 16 x 230.

   a. 31,000
   b. 301,000
   c. 3,100
   d. 3,000,000

5. Below is the attendance for a class of 45.

Day	Number of Absent Students
Monday	5
Tuesday	9
Wednesday	4
Thursday	10
Friday	6

What is the average attendance for the week?

    a. 88%

    b. 85%

    c. 81%

    d. 77%

6. John purchased a jacket at a 7% discount. He had a membership which gave him an additional 2% discount on the discounted price. If he paid $425, what is the retail price of the jacket?

    a. $460

    b. $470

    c. $466

    d. $472

7. Estimate 215 x 65.

    a. 1,350

    b. 13,500

    c. 103,500

    d. 3,500

8. 10 x 2 – (7 + 9)

    a. 21

    b. 16

    c. 4

    d. 13

9. 40% of a number is equal to 90. What is the half of the number?

    a. 18

    b. 112.5

    c. 225

    d. 120

10. 1/4 + 3/10 =

    a. 9/10

    b. 11/20

    c. 7/15

    d. 3/40

11. A map uses a scale of 1:2,000   How much distance on the ground is 5.2 inches on the map if the scale is in inches?

    a. 100,400

    b. 10,500

    c. 10,440

    d. 1,400

12. A shop sells an equipment for $545. If 15% of the cost was added to the price as value added tax, what is the actual cost of the equipment?

    a. $490.40

    b. $473.91

    c. $505.00

    d. $503.15

13. What is 0.27 + 0.33 expressed as a fraction?

    a. 3/6

    b. 4/7

    c. 3/5

    d. 2/7

14. 5 men have to share a load weighing 10 kg 550 g equally among themselves. How much weight will each man have to carry?

    a. 900 g

    b. 1.5 kg

    c. 3 kg

    d. 2 kg 110 g

15. 1/4 + 11/16

    a. 9/16

    b. 1 1/16

    c. 11/16

    d. 15/12

16. A square lawn has an area of 62,500 square meters. What is the cost of building fence around it at a rate of $5.5 per meter?

    a. $4,000

    b. $5,500

    c. $4,500

    d. $5,000

17. A mother is 7 times older than her child. In 25 years, her age will be double that of her child. How old is the mother now?

    a. 35

    b. 33

    c. 30

    d. 25

18. Convert 0.28 to a fraction.

    a. 7/25

    b. 3.25

    c. 8/25

    d. 5/28

19. If a discount of 20% is given for a desk and Mark saves $45, how much did he pay for the desk?

    a. $225

    b. $160

    c. $180

    d. $210

20. In a grade 8 exam, students are asked to divide a number by 3/2, but a student mistakenly multiplied the number by 3/2 and the answer is 5 more than the required one. What was the number?

    a. 4

    b. 5

    c. 6

    d. 8

21. Divide 243 by 3^3

    a. 243

    b. 11

    c. 9

    d. 27

22. Solve the following equation $4(y + 6) = 3y + 30$

    a. $y = 20$

    b. $y = 6$

    c. $y = 30/7$

    d. $y = 30$

23. Divide $x^2 - y^2$ by $x - y$.

    a. $x - y$

    b. $x + y$

    c. xy

    d. $y - x$

24. Solve for x if, $10^2 \times 100^2 = 1000^x$

    a. $x = 2$

    b. $x = 3$

    c. $x = -2$

    d. $x = 0$

25. Given polynomials A = -2x⁴ + x² - 3x, B = x⁴ - x³ + 5 and C = x⁴ + 2x³ + 4x + 5, find A + B - C.

a. $x^3 + x^2 + x + 10$

b. $-3x^3 + x^2 - 7x + 10$

c. $-2x^4 - 3x^3 + x^2 - 7x$

d. $-3x^4 + x^3 + 2 - 7x$

26. Solve the inequality: $(x - 6)^2 \geq x^2 + 12$

a. $(2, + \infty)$

b. $(2, + \infty)$

c. $(-\infty, 2)$

d. $(12, + \infty)$

27. $7^5 - 3^5 =$

a. 15,000

b. 16,564

c. 15,800

d. 15,007

28. Divide $x^3 - 3x^2 + 3x - 1$ by x - 1.

1) $x^2 - 1$

2) $x^2 + 1$

3) $x^2 - 2x + 1$

4) $x^2 + 2x + 1$

29. Express 9 x 9 x 9 in exponential form and standard form.

a. $9^3 = 719$

b. $9^3 = 629$

c. $9^3 = 729$

d. $10^3 = 729$

30. Using the factoring method, solve the quadratic equation: $x^2 - 5x - 6 = 0$

    a. -6 and 1

    b. -1 and 6

    c. 1 and 6

    d. -6 and -1

31. Divide 0.524 by 10^3

    a. 0.0524

    b. 0.00052

    c. 0.00524

    d. 524

32. Factor the polynomial $x^3y^3 - x^2y^8$.

    a. $x^2y^3(x - y^5)$

    b. $x^3y^3(1 - y^5)$

    c. $x^2y^2(x - y^6)$

    d. $xy^3(x - y^5)$

33. Find the solution for the following linear equation:
$5x/2 = 3x + 24/6$

    a. -1

    b. 0

    c. 1

    d. 2

34. $3^2 \times 3^5$

    a. 3^{17}

    b. 3^5

    c. 4^8

    d. 3^7

35. Solve the system, if a is some real number:

ax + y = 1
x + ay = 1

    a. (1,a)

    b. (1/a + 1, 1)

    c. (1/a = 1, 1/a + 1)

    d. (a, 1/a + 1)

36. Solve $3^5 \div 3^8$

    a. 3^3

    b. 3^5

    c. 3^6

    d. 3^4

37. Solve the linear equation: 3(x + 2) - 2(1 - x) = 4x + 5

    a. -1

    b. 0

    c. 1

    d. 2

38. Simplify the following expression: $3x^a + 6a^x - x^a + (-5a^x) - 2x^a$

    a. $a^x + x^a$

    b. $a^x - x^a$

    c. a^x

    d. x^a

39. Add polynomials -3x² + 2x + 6 and -x² - x - 1.

    a. -2x² + x + 5

    b. -4x² + x + 5

    c. -2x² + 3x + 5

    d. -4x² + 3x + 5

40. 10⁴ is not equal to which of the following?

    a. 100,000

    b. 10 x 10 x 10 x 10

    c. 10² x 10²

    d. 10,000

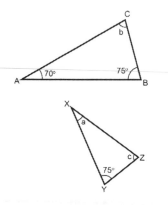

41. What are the respective values of a, b & c if both triangles are similar?

    a. 70°, 70°, 35°

    b. 70°, 35°, 70°

    c. 35°, 35°, 35°

    d. 70°, 35°, 35°

42. For what x is the following equation correct:

$$\log_x 125 = 3$$

a. 1

b. 2

c. 3

d. 5

43. What is the value of the expression $(1 - 4\sin^2(\pi/6))/(1 + 4\cos^2(\pi/3))$?

a. -2

b. -1

c. 0

d. 1/2

44. Calculate $(\sin^2 30^\circ - \sin 0^\circ)/(\cos 90^\circ - \cos 60^\circ)$.

a. -1/2

b. 2/3

c. 0

d. 1/2

45. Consider 2 triangles, ABC and A'B'C', where:

BC = B' C'

AC = A' C'

RA = RA'

Are these 2 triangles congruent?

a. Yes

b. No

c. Not enough information

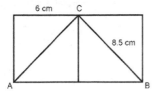

46. What is the perimeter of △ABC in the above shape?

a. 25.5 cm

b. 27 cm

c. 30 cm

d. 29 cm

47. Find the cotangent of a right angle.

a. -1

b. 0

c. 1/2

d. -1/2

48. If angle a is equal to the expression 3π/2 - π/6 - π - π/3, find sina.

a. 0

b. 1/2

c. 1

d. 3/2

49. Find x if $\log_x(9/25) = 2$.

a. 3/5

b. 5/3

c. 6/5

d. 5/6

50. If $a_0 = 1/2$ and an=$2a_{n-1}^2$, find a_2 of the sequence $\{a_n\}$.

   a. 1/2

   b. 1/4

   c. 1/16

   d. 1/24

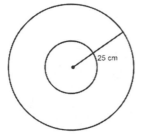

25 cm

51. What is the distance travelled by the wheel above, when it makes 175 revolutions?

   a. 87.5 π m

   b. 875 π m

   c. 8.75 π m

   d. 8750 π m

52. If members of the sequence $\{a_n\}$ are represented by $a_n = (-1)^n a_{n-1}$ and if $a_2 = 2$, find a_0.

   a. 2

   b. 1

   c. 0

   d. -2

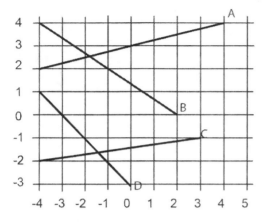

53. Which of the lines above represents the equation 2y – x = 4?

    a. A

    b. B

    c. C

    d. D

54. For any a, find tga/ctga.

    a. -1

    b. 0

    c. 1/2

    d. 1

55. If cosa = 3/5 and b = 24, find side c.

    a. 25

    b. 30

    c. 35

    d. 40

56. Find the sides of a right triangle whose sides are consecutive numbers.

a. 1, 2, 3

b. 2, 3, 4

c. 3, 4, 5

d. 4, 5, 6

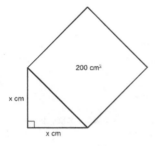

57. What is the length of the sides in the triangle above?

a. 10

b. 20

c. 100

d. 40

58. Calculate $(\cos(\pi/2) + \text{ctg}(\pi/2))/\sin(\pi/2)$.

a. -2

b. -1

c. 0

d. 1/2

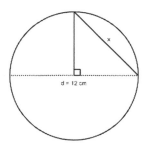

59. Calculate the length of side x.

    a. 6.46

    b. 8.46

    c. 3.6

    d. 6.4

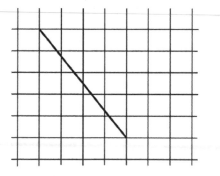

60. What is the slope of the line shown above?

    a. 5/4

    b. -4/5

    c. -5/4

    d. -4/5

Writing Skills

Directions: Select the best option to replace the under-lined portion of the sentence.

1. If Joe had told me the truth, <u>I wouldn't have been</u> so angry.

    a. No change is necessary

    b. If Joe would have told me the truth, I wouldn't have been so angry.

    c. I wouldn't have been so angry if Joe would have told the truth.

    d. If Joe would have telled me the truth, I wouldn't have been so angry.

2. Although you may <u>not see nobody in the dark, it does not mean that not nobody</u> is there.

    a. Although you may not see nobody in the dark, it does not mean that nobody is there.

    b. Although you may not see anyone in the dark, it does not mean that not nobody is there.

    c. Although you may not see anyone in the dark, it does not mean that anyone is there.

    d. No change is necessary.

3. The Ford Motor Company was named for Henry Ford, <u>whom</u> had founded the company.

    a. The Ford Motor Company was named for Henry Ford, which had founded the company.

    b. The Ford Motor Company was named for Henry Ford, who founded the company.

    c. The Ford Motor Company was named for Henry Ford, whose had founded the company.

    d. No change is necessary.

4. Thomas Edison <u>will had been known</u> as the greatest inventor since he invented the light bulb, television, motion pictures, and phonograph.

a. Thomas Edison has always been known as the greatest inventor since he invented the light bulb, television, motion pictures, and phonograph.

b. Thomas Edison was always been known as the greatest inventor since he invented the light bulb, television, motion pictures, and phonograph.

c. Thomas Edison must have had been always known as the greatest inventor since he invented the light bulb, television, motion pictures, and phonograph.

d. No change is necessary.

5. The weatherman on Channel 6 said that this has been <u>the hottest summer</u> on record.

a. The weatherman on Channel 6 said that this has been the most hottest summer on record

b. The weatherman on Channel 6 said that this has been the most hottest summer on record

c. The weatherman on Channel 6 said that this has been the hotter summer on record

d. No change is necessary.

6. Although Joe is tall for his age, his brother Elliot is <u>the tallest of the two</u>.

a. Although Joe is tall for his age, his brother Elliot is more tallest of the two.

b. Although Joe is tall for his age, his brother Elliot is the tall of the two.

c. Although Joe is tall for his age, his brother Elliot is the taller of the two.

d. No change is necessary

7. When KISS came to town, all of the tickets <u>was sold out</u> before I could buy one.

a. When KISS came to town, all of the tickets will be sold out before I could buy one.

b. When KISS came to town, all of the tickets had been sold out before I could buy one.

c. When KISS came to town, all of the tickets were being sold out before I could buy one.

d. No change is necessary.

8. The rules of most sports <u>has been</u> more complicated than we often realize.

a. The rules of most sports are more complicated than we often realize.

b. The rules of most sports is more complicated than we often realize.

c. The rules of most sports was more complicated than we often realize.

d. No change is necessary.

9. Neither of the Wright Brothers <u>had any doubts</u> that they would be successful with their flying machine.

a. Neither of the Wright Brothers have any doubts that they would be successful with their flying machine.

b. Neither of the Wright Brothers has any doubts that they would be successful with their flying machine.

c. Neither of the Wright Brothers will have any doubts that they would be successful with their flying machine.

d. No change is necessary.

10. The Titanic <u>has already sunk</u> mere days into its maiden voyage.

> a. The Titanic will already sunk mere days into its maiden voyage.
>
> b. The Titanic already sank mere days into its maiden voyage.
>
> c. The Titanic sank mere days into its maiden voyage.
>
> d. No change is necessary.

11. To make chicken <u>soup; you </u>must first buy a chicken.

> a. To make chicken soup you must first buy a chicken.
>
> b. To make chicken soup you must first, buy a chicken.
>
> c. To make chicken soup, you must first buy a chicken.
>
> d. None of the choices are correct.

12. To travel around <u>the globe you have </u>to drive 25,000 miles.

> a. To travel around the globe, you have to drive 25000 miles.
>
> b. To travel around the globe, you have to drive, 25000 miles.
>
> c. None of the choices are correct.
>
> d. To travel around the globe, you have to drive 25,000 miles.

13. The dog loved chasing <u>bones; but never ate them:</u> it was running that he enjoyed.

> a. The dog loved chasing bones, but never ate them; it was running that he enjoyed.
>
> b. The dog loved chasing bones; but never ate them, it was running that he enjoyed.
>
> c. The dog loved chasing bones, but never ate them, it was running that he enjoyed.

d. None of the choices are correct.

14. <u>However;</u> I believe that he didn't really try that hard.

    a. However, I believe that he didn't really try that hard.

    b. However I believe that he didn't really try that hard.

    c. None of the choices are correct.

    d. However: I believe that he didn't really try that hard.

15. When he's <u>between</u> friends, Robert seems confident, but, <u>between</u> you and me, he is really shy.

a. None of the choices are correct.

b. When he's among friends, Robert seems confident, but, among you and me, he is really shy.

c. When he's between friends, Robert seems confident, but, among you and me, he is really shy.

d. When he's among friends, Robert seems confident, but, between you and me, he is really shy.

16. I will be finished <u>at about</u> ten in the morning, and will be arriving at home <u>at</u> 6:30.

a. I will be finished at ten in the morning, and will be arriving at home at about 6:30.

b. None of the choices are correct.

c. I will be finished at about ten in the morning, and will be arriving at home at about 6:30.

d. I will be finished at ten in the morning, and will be arriving at home at 6:30.

17. His home was <u>further</u> than we expected; <u>further</u>, the roads were very bad.

    a. His home was farther than we expected; farther, the roads were very bad.

    b. His home was farther than we expected; further, the roads were very bad.

    c. None of the choices are correct.

    d. His home was further than we expected; farther, the roads were very bad.

18. The man was asked to come with <u>her</u> daughter and <u>his</u> test results.

    a. The man was asked to come with his daughter and her test results.

    b. The man was asked to come with her daughter and her test results.

    c. The man was asked to come with her daughter and our test results.

    d. None of the above.

19. The tables were layed by the students.

    a. The tables were laid by the students.

    b. The tables were lay by the students.

    c. The tables were lie by the students.

    d. None of the choices are correct.

20. Each boy and girl <u>were</u> given a toy.

    a. Each boy and girl were given a toy.

    b. Each boy and girl was given a toy.

    c. A and B are correct.

    d. None of the choices are correct.

21. His measles <u>are</u> getting better.

    a. His measles is getting better.

    b. The sentence is correct.

    c. Both of the choices are correct.

    d. None of the choices are correct.

22. In spite of the bad weather yesterday, he <u>can</u> still attend the party.

    a. The sentence is correct.

    b. In spite of the bad weather yesterday, he could still attend the party.

    c. In spite of the bad weather yesterday, he may still attend the party.

    d. None of the choices are correct.

23. Any girl that fails the test loses <u>her</u> admission.

    a. Any girl that fails the test loses their admission.

    b. Any girl that fails the test loses our admission.

    c. The sentence is correct.

    d. None of the choices are correct.

24. He <u>ought</u> be back by now.

    a. He ought to be back by now.

    b. The sentence is correct.

    c. He ought come back by now.

    d. None of the choices are correct.

25. The man as well as his son <u>have</u> arrived.

    a. The man as well as his son has arrived

    b. The sentence is correct.

    c. None of the choices are correct.

26. Mark and Peter have talked <u>to each other</u>.

   a. The sentence is correct.

   b. Mark and Peter have talked to one another.

   c. None of the choices are correct.

27. Christians believe that their lord <u>have</u> raise.

   a. Christians believe that their lord have raised.

   b. Christians believe that their lord has risen.

   c. The sentence is correct.

   d. None of the choices are correct.

28. Here are the names of people <u>whom</u> you should contact.

   a. The sentence is correct.

   b. Here are the names of people who you should contact

   c. None of the choices are correct.

29. The World Health Organization (WHO) <u>are</u> meeting by January.

   a. The sentence is correct.

   b. The World Health Organization (WHO) is meeting by January.

   c. None of the choices are correct.

30. They <u>shall</u> have to retire when they reach 60 years of age.

   a. They will have to retire when they reach 60 years of age.

   b. The sentence is correct.

   c. None of the choices are correct.

Answer Key

Reading

1. B
We can infer from this passage that sickness from an infectious disease can be easily transmitted from one person to another.

From the passage, "Infectious pathologies are also called communicable diseases or transmissible diseases, due to their potential of transmission from one person or species to another by a replicating agent (as opposed to a toxin)."

2. A
Two other names for infectious pathologies are communicable diseases and transmissible diseases.

From the passage, "Infectious pathologies are also called communicable diseases or transmissible diseases, due to their potential of transmission from one person or species to another by a replicating agent (as opposed to a toxin)."

3. C
Infectivity describes the ability of an organism to enter, survive and multiply in the host. This is taken directly from the passage, and is a definition type question.

Definition type questions can be answered quickly and easily by scanning the passage for the word you are asked to define.

"Infectivity" is an unusual word, so it is quick and easy to scan the passage looking for this word.

4. B
We know an infection is not synonymous with an infectious disease because an infection may not cause important clinical symptoms or impair host function.

5. C
The cumulus stage of a thunderstorm is the beginning of the

thunderstorm.

This is taken directly from the passage, "The first stage of a thunderstorm is the cumulus, or developing stage."

6. D
The passage lists four ways that air is heated. One of the ways is, heat created by water vapor condensing into liquid.

7. A
The sequence of events can be taken from these sentences:

As the moisture carried by the [1] air currents rises, it rapidly cools into liquid drops of water, which appear as cumulus clouds. As the water vapor condenses into liquid, it [2] releases heat, which warms the air. This in turn causes the air to become less dense than the surrounding dry air and [3] rise further.

8. C
The purpose of this text is to explain when meteorologists consider a thunderstorm severe.

The main idea is the first sentence, "The United States National Weather Service classifies thunderstorms as severe when they reach a predetermined level." After the first sentence, the passage explains and elaborates on this idea. Everything is this passage is related to this idea, and there are no other major ideas in this passage that are central to the whole passage.

9. A
From this passage, we can infer that different areas and countries have different criteria for determining a severe storm.

From the passage we can see that most of the US has a criteria of, winds over 50 knots (58 mph or 93 km/h), and hail ¾ inch (2 cm). For the Central US, hail must be 1 inch (2.5 cm) in diameter. In Canada, winds must be 90 km/h or greater, hail 2 centimeters in diameter or greater, and rainfall more than 50 millimeters in 1 hour, or 75 millimeters in 3 hours.

Option D is incorrect because the Canadian system is the same for hail, 2 centimeters in diameter.

10. C
With hail above the minimum size of 2.5 cm. diameter, the Central Region of the United States National Weather Service would issue a severe thunderstorm warning.

11. D
Clouds in space are made of different materials attracted by gravity. Clouds on Earth are made of water droplets or ice crystals.

Choice D is the best answer. Notice also that Choice D is the most specific.

12. C
The main idea is the first sentence of the passage; a cloud is a visible mass of droplets or frozen crystals floating in the atmosphere above the surface of the Earth or other planetary body.

The main idea is very often the first sentence of the paragraph.

13. C
This question asks about the process, and gives options that can be confirmed or eliminated easily.

From the passage, "Dense, deep clouds reflect most light, so they appear white, at least from the top. Cloud droplets scatter light very efficiently, so the further into a cloud light travels, the weaker it gets. This accounts for the gray or dark appearance at the base of large clouds."

We can eliminate choice A, since water droplets inside the cloud do not reflect light is false.

We can eliminate choice B, since, water droplets outside the cloud reflect light, it appears dark, is false.

Choice C is correct.

14. B
The general tone is informal.

15. B
The statement, " Fewer people have aquariums in their office than at home," cannot be inferred from this article.

16. C
The author does not provide evidence for this statement.

17. B
The following statement is an opinion, " Aquarium gravel improves the aesthetics of the aquarium."

18. D
This question tests the reader's summarization skills. The question is asking very generally about the message of the passage, and the title, "Ways Characters Communicate in Theater", is one indication of that. The other answers A, B, and C are all directly from the text, and therefore readers may be inclined to select one of them, but are too specific to encapsulate the entirety of the passage and its message.

19. B
The paragraph on soliloquies mentions "To be or not to be", and it is from the context of that paragraph that readers may understand that because "To be or not to be" is a soliloquy, Hamlet will be introspective, or thoughtful, while delivering it. It is true that actors deliver soliloquies alone, and may be "solitary" (A), but "thoughtful" (B) is more true to the overall idea of the paragraph. Readers may choose C because drama and theater can be used interchangeably and the passage mentions that soliloquies are unique to theater (and therefore drama), but this answer is not specific enough to the paragraph in question. Readers may pick up on the theme of life and death and Hamlet's true intentions and select that he is "hopeless" (D), but those themes are not discussed either by this paragraph or passage, as a close textual reading and analysis confirms.

20. C
This question tests the reader's grammatical skills. B seems logical, but parenthesis are actually considered to be a stronger break in a sentence than commas are, and along this line of thinking, actually disrupt the sentence more. A and D make comparisons between theater and film that are simply not made in the passage, and may or may not be true. This detail does clarify the statement that asides are most unique to theater by adding that it is not completely unique to theater, which may have been why the author didn't chose not to delete it and instead used parentheses to designate the detail's importance (C).

Mathematics

1. C
If there are 5 friends and each drink costs $1.89, we can round up to $2 per drink and estimate the total cost at, 5 X $2 = $10.
The actual cost is 5 X $1.89 = $9.45.

2. D
If we subtract 25 pounds from the total 205, then in remaining 180 pounds, their weights are equal, at 90 pounds each. So Sarah's weight will be = 90 + 25 = 115 pounds.

In kilograms it will be = 115×0.4535 = 52.15 Kg.
Sarah will weigh approximately 52 Kg.

3. D
$75/1500 = 15/300 = 3/60 = 1/20$

4. C
16 X 230 is about 3,100. The actual number is 3680.

5. B

Day	Number of Absent Students	Number of Present Students	% Attendance
Monday	5	40	88.88%
Tuesday	9	36	80.00%
Wednesday	4	41	91.11%
Thursday	10	35	77.77%
Friday	6	39	86.66%

To find the average or mean, sum the series and divide by the number of items.
88.88 + 80.00 + 91.11 + 77.77 + 86.66/5
424.42/5 = 84.88
Round up to 85%.

Percentage attendance will be 85%

6. C
Let the original price be x, then at the rate of 7% the discounted price will be = 0.93x. 2% discounted amount then will be = 0.02 × 0.93x = 0.0186x. Remaining price = 0.93x - 0.0186x = 0.9114x. This is the amount which John has paid so 0.9114x = 425. X = 425/0.9114. Solving for X = 466.31

7. B
215 X 65 is about 13,500. The exact answer is 13,975.

8. C
10 x 2 – (7 + 9) . This is an order of operations question. Do brackets first, then multiplication and division, then addition and subtraction.

10 x 2 - 16
20 - 16 = 4.

9. B
40/100 X = 90
40X = (90 * 100) = 9000
x = 9000/40 = 900/4 = 225
Half of 225 = 112.5

10. B
First, see if you can eliminate any choices. 1/4 + 1/3 is going to equal about 1/2.

Choice A, 9/10 is very close to 1, so it can be eliminated.
Choices B and C are very close to 1/2 so they should be considered.
Choice D is less than half and very close to zero, so it can be eliminated.

Looking at the denominators, Choice C has denominator of 15, and Choice B has denominator of 20. Right away, notice that 20 is common multiple of 4 and 10, and 15 is not.

11. C
1 inch on map = 2,000 inches on ground. So 5.2 inches on map = 5.2 x 2,000 = 10,440 inches on ground.

12. B
Actual cost = X, therefore, 545 = x + 0.15x, 545 = 1x + 0.15x, 545 = 1.15x, x = 545/1.15 = 473.9

13. C
0.27 + 0.33 = 0.60 and 0.60 = 60/100 = 3/5

14. D
First convert all units to grams. Since 1000 g = 1 kg, 10 kg = 10 x 1000 = 10,000 + 550 g = 10,550 g. Divide 10,550 among 5 = 10550/5 = 2110 = 2 kg 110 g

15. D
A common denominator is needed, a number which both 4 and 16 will divide into. So, 4+11/16 = 15/16

16. B
As the lawn is square, the length of one side will be the squre root of the area. √62,500 = 250 meters. So the perimeters will be 250 × 4 = 1000 meters. The total cost will be 1000 × 5.5 = $5500.

17. A
Suppose the mother's age is x years and the child's is y. Then y = 7x. After 25 years, y + 25 = 2(x + 25). Solving for y, y + 25 = 2x + 50. Putting the value of y = 7x in the below

equation $7x + 25 = 2x + 50$. Solving for x = 5 years. So child is 5 years old and mother is 35.

18. A
$0.28 = 28/100 = 7/25$

19. A
$20/100 = 45/x$
$20x = 4500$
$x = 4500/20 = 450/2 = 225$

20. C
Let the number be x. $(x * 3/2) – (x / 3/2) = 5$
$X = 6$

21. C
$243/3 \times 3 \times 3 = 243/27 = 9$

22. B
$4y + 24 = 3y + 30$, $= 4y – 3y + 24 = 30$, $= y + 24 = 30$, $= y = 30 – 24$, $= y = 6$

23. B
$(x^2 - y^2) / (x - y) = x + y$

$$\frac{-(x^2 - xy)}{xy - y^2}$$

$$\frac{-(xy - y^2)}{0}$$

24. A
$10 \times 10 \times 100 \times 100 = 1000^x$, $=100 \times 10,000 = 1000^x$, $= 1,000,000 = 1000^x = x = 2$

25. C
$A + B - C = (-2x^4 + x^2 - 3x) + (x^4 - x^3 + 5) - (x^4 + 2x^3 + 4x + 5)$
$-2x^4 + x^2 - 3x + x^4 - x^3 + 5 - x^4 - 2x^3 - 4x - 5$
$-2x^4 - 3x^3 + x^2 - 7x$

26. C
$(x - 6)^2 \geq x^2 + 12$
$x^2 - 12x + 36 \geq x^2 + 12$
$-12x \geq 12 - 36$

-12x ≥ -24
-x ≥ -2/-1
x ≤ 2
27. B
(7 x 7 x 7 x 7 x 7) - (3 x 3 x 3 x 3 x 3) = 16,807 – 243 =
16,564.

28. C
$(x^3 - 3x^2 + 3x - 1) / (x - 1) = x^2 - 2x + 1$
-$\underline{(x^3 - x^2)}$
 -2x² + 3x - 1
 $\underline{-(-2 x^2 + 2x)}$
   x - 1

$\underline{-(x - 1)}$
0

29. C
Exponential form is 9^3 and standard from is 729
30. B
x² - 5x - 6 = 0
x² - 6x + x - 6 = 0
x(x - 6) + x - 6 = 0
(x - 6)(x + 1) = 0
(x = 6) U (x = -1)

31. B
0.524/ 10 x 10 x 10 = 0.524/1000 = 0.000524

32. A
$x^3y^3 - x^2y^8 = x *(x^2y^3 - x^2y^3 * y^5 = x^2y^3(x - y^5)$

33. D
5x/2 = 3x + 24/6
3 * 5x/3 * 2 = 3x + 24/6
15x/6 = 3x + 24/6
15x = 3x + 24
15x - 3x = 25
12x = 24
x = 24/12 = 2

34. D
When multiplying exponents with the same base, add the

exponents. $3^2 \times 3^5 = 3^{2+5} = 3^7$

35. C
$y = 1 - ax$
$x + a(1 - ax) = 1$
$x + a - a^2x = 1$
$x(1 - a^2) = 1 - a$
$x = 1 - a/1 = a^2 = 1 - a/(1 - a)(1 + a) = 1/a + 1$

$y = 1 - ax$
$y = 1 - a * 1/a + 1 = a/a + 1$
$y = a + 1 - a/a + 1 = 1/a + 1$

36. A
To divide exponents with the same base, subtract the exponents. $3^{8-5} = 3^3$

37. C
$3(x + 2) - 2(1 - x) = 4x + 5$
$3x + 6 - 2 + 2x = 4x + 5$
$5x + 4 = 4x + 5$
$5x - 4x = 5 - 4$
$x = 1$

38. C
$3x^a + 6a^x - x^a + (-5a^x) - 2x^a = 3x^a + 6a^x - x^a - 5a^x - 2x^a = a^x$

39. B
$-4x^2 + x + 5$
$(-3x^2 + 2x + 6) + (-x^2 - x - 1)$
$-3x^2 + 2x + 6 -x^2 - x - 1$
$-4x^2 + x + 5$

40. A
10^4 is not equal to 100,000
$10^4 = 10 \times 10 \times 10 \times 10 = 10^2 \times 10^2 = 10,000$

41. D
Comparing angles on similar triangles, a, b and c will be 70°, 35°, 35°

42. D
$\log_x 125 = 3$

$x^3 = 125$
$x^3 = 5^3$
$x = 5$

43. C
$(1 - 4\sin^2(\pi/6))/(1+4\cos^2(\pi/3)) =$
$(1 - 4\sin^2(30^0))/(1 + 4\cos^2(60^0))$
$(1 - 4(1/2)^2)/(1 + 4(1/2)^2)$
$(1 - 4(1/4))/(1 + 4(1/4))$
$(1 - 1)/(1 + 1) = 0/2 = 0$

44. A
$(\sin^2 30^0 - \sin 0^0)/(\cos 90^0 - \cos 60^0) =$
$((1/2)\,2 - 0)\,/\,(0-1/2)$
$(1/4)\,/\,(-1/2) = -1/2$

45. A
Yes the triangles are congruent.

46. D
Perimeter of triangle ABC within two squares.
Perimeter = sum of the sides.
Perimeter = 8.5 + 8.5 + 6 + 6
Perimeter = 29 cm.

47. B
$a=90^0$
$\text{ctg}90^0 = \cos 90^0/\sin 90^0 = 0/1 = 0$

48. A
$a = 3\pi/2 - \pi/6 - \pi - \pi/3$
$(9\pi - \pi - 6\pi - 2\pi)/6$
$0\pi/6 = 0$
$\sin a = \sin 0^0 = 0$

49. A
$\log_x(9/25) = 2$
$x^2 = 9/25$
$x^2 = (3/5)^2$
$x = 3/5$

50. A
$a_0 = 1/2$

$a_n = 2a_{n-1}^2$
$a_1 = 2a_0^2 = 2 * (1/2)^2 = 2 * (1/4) = 1/2$
$a_2 = 2a_1^2 = 2 * (1/2)^2 = 2 * (1/4) = 1/2$

51. A
Diameter = 2 x radius.
Circumference = π x Diameter

Distance(meters) = (Circumference x Revolutions)/100
Distance(meters) = [((25 x 2) π) x 175]/100
Distance(meters) = 8750 π/100
Distance = 87.5 π meters.

52. D
$a_n = (-1)^n a_{n-1}$
$a_2 = 2$
$2 = a_2 = (-1)^2 a_1 = a_1 \rightarrow a_1 = 2$
$a_1 = (-1)^1 a_0$
$2 = -a_0$
$a_0 = -2$

53. A
Line A represents the equation 2y – x = 4.

54. D
tga/ctga = (sina/cosa)/(cosa/sina) = 1
or
tga/ctga = (a/b)/(b/a) = ab/ab = 1

55. D
cosa = 3/5 = b/c
b = 24
3/5 = b/c
3/5 = 24/c
3c = 5 *24
c = 40

56. C
The length of the sides is, 3, 4, 5.
x
y = x + 1
z = x + 2
$x^2 + y^2 = y^2$

$x^2 + (x + 1)^2 = (x + 2)^2$

$x^2 + x^2 + 2x + 1 = x^2 + 4x + 4$

$x^2 - 2x - 3 \ 0$

$x_{1,2} = 2 \pm \sqrt{4} + 12 \ / \ 2$

$x_{1,2} = 2 \pm 4 \ / \ 2$

$x = 3$

$y = 4$

$z = 5$

57. A
Pythagorean Theorem:

$(\text{Hypotenuse})^2 = (\text{Perpendicular})^2 + (\text{Base})^2$

$h^2 = a^2 + b^2$

Given: $h^2 = 200$, $a = b = x$

Then, $x^2 + x^2 = 200$, $2x^2 = 200$, $x^2 = 100$

$x = 10$

58. C
$(\cos(\pi/2) + \text{ctg}(\pi/2))/\sin(\pi/2) = (\cos 90^0 + \text{ctg} 90^0)/\sin 90^0 = (0+0)/1 = 0$

59. B
Pythagorean Theorem:

$(\text{Hypotenuse})^2 = (\text{Perpendicular})^2 + (\text{Base})^2$

$h^2 = a^2 + b^2$

Given: d (diameter)= 12 & r (radius) = a = b = 6

$h^2 = a^2 + b^2$

$h^2 = 6^2 + 6^2$, $h^2 = 36 + 36$

$h^2 = 72$

$h = 8.46$

60. C
Slope (m) = <u>change in y</u>
                          change in x

$(x_1, y_1)=(-3,1)$ & $(x_2, y_2)= (1,-4)$

Slope = $[-4 - 1]/[1-(-3)] = -5/4$

Writing Skills

1. A
The third conditional is used for talking about an unreal situation (that did not happen) in the past. For example, "If I had studied harder, [if clause] I would have passed the exam [main clause]. Which is the same as, "I failed the exam, because I didn't study hard enough."

2. C
Double negative sentence. In double negative sentences, one of the negatives is replaced with "any."

3. B
The sentence refers to a person, so "who" is the only correct option.

4. A
The sentence requires the past perfect "has always been known." Furthermore, this is the only grammatically correct choice.

5. B
The superlative, "hottest," is used when expressing a temperature greater than that of anything to which it is being compared.

6. D
When comparing two items, use "the taller." When comparing more than two items, use "the tallest."

7. B
The past perfect form is used to describe an event that occurred in the past and prior to another event.

8. A
The subject is "rules" so the present tense plural form, "are," is used to agree with "realize."

9. C
The simple past tense, "had," is correct because it refers to completed action in the past.

10. C
The simple past tense, "sank," is correct because it refers to completed action in the past.

11. C
Comma separate phrases.

12. D
The comma separates clauses and numbers are separated with a comma. The correct sentence is,
'To travel around the globe, you have to drive 25,000 miles.'

13. A
The dog loved chasing bones, but never ate them; it was running that he enjoyed.

14. A
When using 'however,' place a comma before and after, except when however begins the sentence.

15. D
Among vs. Between. 'Among' is for more than 2 items, and 'between' is only for 2 items.

When he's among friends (many or more than 2), Robert seems confident, but, between you and me (two), he is very shy.

16. D
At vs. About. At refers to a specific time and about refers to a more general time. A common usage is 'at about 10,' but it isn't proper grammar.

17. B
Further vs. Farther. 'Farther' is used for physical distance, and 'further' is used for figurative distance.

18. A
A Pronoun should conform to its antecedent in gender, number and person.

19. A
The verb LAY should always take an object. Here the subject is the table. The three forms of the verb lay are: lay, laid and laid. The sentence above is in past tense.

20. B
Use the singular verb form when nouns are qualified with "every" or "each," even if they are joined by 'and. '

21. B
The sentence is correct. Use a plural verb for nouns like measles, tongs, trousers, riches, scissors etc.

22. B
Use "could," the past tense of "can" to express ability or capacity.

23. C
The sentence is correct. Words such as neither, each, many, either, every, everyone, everybody and any should take a singular pronoun.

24. A
The verb "ought" can be used to express desirability, duty and probability. The verb is usually followed by "to."

25. A
When two subjects are linked with "with" or "as well," use the verb form that matches the first subject.

26. A
When you use 'each other' it should be used for two things or people. When you use 'one another' it should be used for things and people above two

27. B
The verb rise ('to go up', 'to ascend.') can appear in three forms, rise, rose, and risen. The verb should not take an object.

28. A
The sentence is correct. Use "whom" in the objective case, and use "who" a subjective case.

29. B
Use a singular verb with a proper noun in plural form that refers to a single entity. Here the The World Health Organization is a single entity, although it is made up on many members.

30. A

Will is used in the second or third person (they, he, she and you), while shall is used in the first person (I and we). Both verbs are used to express futurity.

Practice Test Questions Set 2

The questions below are not exactly the same as you will find on the COMPASS® - that would be too easy! And nobody knows what the questions will be and they change all the time. Below are general questions that cover the same subject areas as the COMPASS®. So while the format and exact wording of the questions may differ slightly, and change from year to year, if you can answer the questions below, you will have no problem with the COMPASS®.

For the best results, take these Practice Test Questions as if it were the real exam. Set aside time when you will not be disturbed, and a location that is quiet and free of distractions. Read the instructions carefully, read each question carefully, and answer to the best of your ability.
Use the bubble answer sheets provided. When you have completed the Practice Questions, check your answer against the Answer Key and read the explanation provided.

Do not attempt more than one set of practice test questions in one day. After completing the first practice test, wait two or three days before attempting the second set of questions.

Reading Answer Sheet

1. Ⓐ Ⓑ Ⓒ Ⓓ   11. Ⓐ Ⓑ Ⓒ Ⓓ   21. Ⓐ Ⓑ Ⓒ Ⓓ

2. Ⓐ Ⓑ Ⓒ Ⓓ   12. Ⓐ Ⓑ Ⓒ Ⓓ   22. Ⓐ Ⓑ Ⓒ Ⓓ

3. Ⓐ Ⓑ Ⓒ Ⓓ   13. Ⓐ Ⓑ Ⓒ Ⓓ   23. Ⓐ Ⓑ Ⓒ Ⓓ

4. Ⓐ Ⓑ Ⓒ Ⓓ   14. Ⓐ Ⓑ Ⓒ Ⓓ   24. Ⓐ Ⓑ Ⓒ Ⓓ

5. Ⓐ Ⓑ Ⓒ Ⓓ   15. Ⓐ Ⓑ Ⓒ Ⓓ   25. Ⓐ Ⓑ Ⓒ Ⓓ

6. Ⓐ Ⓑ Ⓒ Ⓓ   16. Ⓐ Ⓑ Ⓒ Ⓓ   26. Ⓐ Ⓑ Ⓒ Ⓓ

7. Ⓐ Ⓑ Ⓒ Ⓓ   17. Ⓐ Ⓑ Ⓒ Ⓓ   27. Ⓐ Ⓑ Ⓒ Ⓓ

8. Ⓐ Ⓑ Ⓒ Ⓓ   18. Ⓐ Ⓑ Ⓒ Ⓓ   28. Ⓐ Ⓑ Ⓒ Ⓓ

9. Ⓐ Ⓑ Ⓒ Ⓓ   19. Ⓐ Ⓑ Ⓒ Ⓓ   29. Ⓐ Ⓑ Ⓒ Ⓓ

10. Ⓐ Ⓑ Ⓒ Ⓓ   20. Ⓐ Ⓑ Ⓒ Ⓓ   30. Ⓐ Ⓑ Ⓒ Ⓓ

Mathematics Answer Sheet

1. (A) (B) (C) (D)   21. (A) (B) (C) (D)   41. (A) (B) (C) (D)

2. (A) (B) (C) (D)   22. (A) (B) (C) (D)   42. (A) (B) (C) (D)

3. (A) (B) (C) (D)   23. (A) (B) (C) (D)   43. (A) (B) (C) (D)

4. (A) (B) (C) (D)   24. (A) (B) (C) (D)   44. (A) (B) (C) (D)

5. (A) (B) (C) (D)   25. (A) (B) (C) (D)   45. (A) (B) (C) (D)

6. (A) (B) (C) (D)   26. (A) (B) (C) (D)   46. (A) (B) (C) (D)

7. (A) (B) (C) (D)   27. (A) (B) (C) (D)   47. (A) (B) (C) (D)

8. (A) (B) (C) (D)   28. (A) (B) (C) (D)   48. (A) (B) (C) (D)

9. (A) (B) (C) (D)   29. (A) (B) (C) (D)   49. (A) (B) (C) (D)

10. (A) (B) (C) (D)   30. (A) (B) (C) (D)   50. (A) (B) (C) (D)

11. (A) (B) (C) (D)   31. (A) (B) (C) (D)   51. (A) (B) (C) (D)

12. (A) (B) (C) (D)   32. (A) (B) (C) (D)   52. (A) (B) (C) (D)

13. (A) (B) (C) (D)   33. (A) (B) (C) (D)   53. (A) (B) (C) (D)

14. (A) (B) (C) (D)   34. (A) (B) (C) (D)   54. (A) (B) (C) (D)

15. (A) (B) (C) (D)   35. (A) (B) (C) (D)   55. (A) (B) (C) (D)

16. (A) (B) (C) (D)   36. (A) (B) (C) (D)   56. (A) (B) (C) (D)

17. (A) (B) (C) (D)   37. (A) (B) (C) (D)   57. (A) (B) (C) (D)

18. (A) (B) (C) (D)   38. (A) (B) (C) (D)   58. (A) (B) (C) (D)

19. (A) (B) (C) (D)   39. (A) (B) (C) (D)   59. (A) (B) (C) (D)

20. (A) (B) (C) (D)   40. (A) (B) (C) (D)   60. (A) (B) (C) (D)

Writing Skills Answer Sheet

1. (A) (B) (C) (D) 11. (A) (B) (C) (D) 21. (A) (B) (C) (D)

2. (A) (B) (C) (D) 12. (A) (B) (C) (D) 22. (A) (B) (C) (D)

3. (A) (B) (C) (D) 13. (A) (B) (C) (D) 23. (A) (B) (C) (D)

4. (A) (B) (C) (D) 14. (A) (B) (C) (D) 24. (A) (B) (C) (D)

5. (A) (B) (C) (D) 15. (A) (B) (C) (D) 25. (A) (B) (C) (D)

6. (A) (B) (C) (D) 16. (A) (B) (C) (D) 26. (A) (B) (C) (D)

7. (A) (B) (C) (D) 17. (A) (B) (C) (D) 27. (A) (B) (C) (D)

8. (A) (B) (C) (D) 18. (A) (B) (C) (D) 28. (A) (B) (C) (D)

9. (A) (B) (C) (D) 19. (A) (B) (C) (D) 29. (A) (B) (C) (D)

10. (A) (B) (C) (D) 20. (A) (B) (C) (D) 30. (A) (B) (C) (D)

Part 1 – Reading and Language Arts

Questions 1 - 4 refer to the following passage.

The Respiratory System

The respiratory system's function is to allow oxygen exchange through all parts of the body. The anatomy or structure of the exchange system, and the uses of the exchanged gases, varies depending on the organism. In humans and other mammals, for example, the anatomical features of the respiratory system include airways, lungs, and the respiratory muscles. Molecules of oxygen and carbon dioxide are passively exchanged, by diffusion, between the gaseous external environment and the blood. This exchange process occurs in the alveolar region of the lungs.

Other animals, such as insects, have respiratory systems with very simple anatomical features, and in amphibians even the skin plays a vital role in gas exchange. Plants also have respiratory systems but the direction of gas exchange can be opposite to that of animals.

The respiratory system can also be divided into physiological, or functional, zones. These include the conducting zone (the region for gas transport from the outside atmosphere to just above the alveoli), the transitional zone, and the respiratory zone (the alveolar region where gas exchange occurs). [8]

1. What can we infer from the first paragraph in this passage?

    a. Human and mammal respiratory systems are the same.

    b. The lungs are an important part of the respiratory system.

    c. The respiratory system varies in different mammals.

    d. Oxygen and carbon dioxide are passive exchanged by the respiratory system.

2. What is the process by which molecules of oxygen and carbon dioxide are passively exchanged?

    a. Transfusion

    b. Affusion

    c. Diffusion

    d. Respiratory confusion

3. What organ plays an important role in gas exchange in amphibians?

    a. The skin

    b. The lungs

    c. The gills

    d. The mouth

4. What are the three physiological zones of the respiratory system?

    a. Conducting, transitional, respiratory zones

    b. Redacting, transitional, circulatory zones

    c. Conducting, circulatory, inhibiting zones

    d. Transitional, inhibiting, conducting zones

Questions 5 - 8 refer to the following passage.

Lightning

Lightning is an electrical discharge that occurs in a thunderstorm. Often you'll see it in the form of a bright "bolt" (or streak) coming from the sky. Lightning occurs when static electricity inside clouds builds up and causes an electrical charge. What causes the static electricity? Water! Specifically, water droplets collide with ice crystals after the temperature in the cloud falls below freezing. Sometimes these collisions are small, but other times they're quite large. Large collisions cause large electrical charges, and when they're large enough, look out! The hyper-charged cloud will emit a burst of lightning. This lightning looks quite impressive. For a good reason, too: A lightning bolt's temperature gets so hot that it's sometimes five times hotter than the sun's surface. Although the lightning bolt is hot, it's also short-lived. Because of that, when a person is unfortunate enough to be struck by lightning, their odds of surviving are pretty good. Statistics show that 90% of victims survive a lightning blast. Oh, and that old saying, "Lightning never strikes twice in the same spot"? It's a myth! Many people report surviving lightning blasts three or more times. What's more, lightning strikes some skyscrapers multiple times. The other prominent feature of lightning storms is the thunder. This is caused by the super-heated air around a lightning bolt expands at the speed of sound. We hear thunder after seeing the lightning bolt because sound travels slower than the speed of light. In reality, though, both occur at the same moment.

5. What can we infer from this passage?

    a. An electrical discharge in the clouds causes lightning.

    b. Lightning is not as hot as the temperature of the sun's surface.

    c. The sound that lightning makes occurs when electricity strikes an object.

    d. We hear lightning before we see it.

6. Being struck by lightning means:

    a. Instant death.

    b. Less than a fifty percent chance of survival.

    c. A ninety percent chance of surviving the strike.

    d. An eighty percent chance of survival.

7. Lightning is caused by the following:

    a. Water droplets colliding with ice crystals creating static electricity.

    b. Friction from the clouds rubbing together.

    c. Water droplets colliding.

    d. Warm and cold air mixing together.

Questions 8 - 11 refer to the following passage.

Low Blood Sugar

As the name suggest, low blood sugar is low sugar levels in the bloodstream. This can occur when you have not eaten properly and undertake strenuous activity, or when you are very hungry. When Low blood sugar occurs regularly and is ongoing, it is a medical condition called hypoglycemia. This condition can occur in diabetics and also in healthy adults.

Causes of low blood sugar can include excessive alcohol consumption, metabolic problems, stomach surgery, pancreas, liver or kidneys problems, as well as a side-effect of some medications.

Symptoms

There are different symptoms depending on the severity of the case.

Mild hypoglycemia can lead to feelings of nausea and hunger. The patient may also feel nervous, jittery and have fast heart beats. Sweaty skin, clammy and cold skin are likely symptoms.

Moderate hypoglycemia can result in a short temper, confusion, nervousness, fear and blurring of vision. The patient may feel weak and unsteady.

Severe cases of hypoglycemia can lead to seizures, coma, fainting spells, nightmares, headaches, excessive sweats and severe tiredness.

Diagnosis of low blood sugar

A doctor can diagnosis this medical condition by asking the patient questions and testing blood and urine samples. Home testing kits are available for patients to monitor blood sugar levels. It is important to see a qualified doctor though. The doctor can administer tests to ensure that will safely rule out other medical conditions that could affect blood sugar levels.

Treatment

Quick treatments include drinking or eating foods and drinks with high sugar contents. Good examples include soda, fruit juice, hard candy and raisins. Glucose energy tablets can also help. Doctors may also recommend medications and well as changes in diet and exercise routine to treat chronic low blood sugar.

8. Based on the article, which of the following is true?

    a. Low blood sugar can happen to anyone.

    b. Low blood sugar only happens to diabetics.

    c. Low blood sugar can occur even.

    d. None of the statements are true.

9. Which of the following are the author's opinion?

    a. Quick treatments include drinking or eating foods and drinks with high sugar contents.

    b. None of the statements are opinions.

    c. This condition can occur in diabetics and also in healthy adults.

    d. There are different symptoms depending on the severity of the case

10. What is the author's purpose?

    a. To inform

    b. To persuade

    c. To entertain

    d. To analyze

11. Which of the following is not a detail?

    a. A doctor can diagnosis this medical condition by asking the patient questions and testing.

    b. A doctor will test blood and urine samples.

    c. Glucose energy tablets can also help.

    d. Home test kits monitor blood sugar levels.

Questions 12 - 15 refer to the following passage.

Myths, Legend and Folklore

Cultural historians draw a distinction between myth, legend and folktale simply as a way to group traditional stories. However, in many cultures, drawing a sharp line between myths and legends is not that simple. Instead of dividing their traditional stories into myths, legends, and folktales, some cultures divide them into two categories. The first category roughly corresponds to folktales, and the second is one that combines myths and legends. Similarly, we can not always separate myths from folktales. One society might consider a story true, making it a myth. Another society may believe the story is fiction, which makes it a folktale. In fact, when a myth loses its status as part of a religious system, it often takes on traits more typical of folktales, with its formerly divine characters now appearing as human heroes, giants, or fairies. Myth, legend, and folktale are only a few of the categories of traditional stories. Other categories include anecdotes and some kinds of jokes. Traditional stories, in turn, are only one category within the much larger category of folklore, which also includes items such as gestures, costumes, and music. [9]

12. The main idea of this passage is that

a. Myths, fables, and folktales are not the same thing, and each describes a specific type of story

b. Traditional stories can be categorized in different ways by different people

c. Cultures use myths for religious purposes, and when this is no longer true, the people forget and discard these myths

d. Myths can never become folk tales, because one is true, and the other is false

13. The terms myth and legend are

a. Categories that are synonymous with true and false

b. Categories that group traditional stories according to certain characteristics

c. Interchangeable, because both terms mean a story that is passed down from generation to generation

d. Meant to distinguish between a story that involves a hero and a cultural message and a story meant only to entertain

14. Traditional story categories not only include myths and legends, but

a. Can also include gestures, since some cultures passed these down before the written and spoken word

b. In addition, folklore refers to stories involving fables and fairy tales

c. These story categories can also include folk music and traditional dress

d. Traditional stories themselves are a part of the larger category of folklore, which may also include costumes, gestures, and music

15. This passage shows that

> a. There is a distinct difference between a myth and a legend, although both are folktales
>
> b. Myths are folktales, but folktales are not myths
>
> c. Myths, legends, and folktales play an important part in tradition and the past, and are a rich and colorful part of history
>
> d. Most cultures consider myths to be true

Questions 16 - 18 refer to the following passage.

How To Get A Good Nights Sleep

Sleep is just as essential for healthy living as water, air and food. Sleep allows the body to rest and replenish depleted energy levels. Sometimes we may for various reasons experience difficulty sleeping which has a serious effect on our health. Those who have prolonged sleeping problems are facing a serious medical condition and should see a qualified doctor as soon as possible for help. Here is simple guide that can help you sleep better at night.

Try to create a natural pattern of waking up and sleeping around the same time everyday. This means avoiding going to bed too early and oversleeping past your usual wake up time. Going to bed and getting up at radically different times everyday confuses your body clock. Try to establish a natural rhythm as much as you can.

Exercises and a bit of physical activity can help you sleep better at night. If you are having problem sleeping, try to be as active as you can during the day. If you are tired from physical activity, falling asleep is a natural and easy process for your body. If you remain inactive during the day, you will find it harder to sleep properly at night. Try walking, jogging, swimming or simple stretches as you get close to your bed time.

Afternoon naps are great to refresh you during the day, but

they may also keep you awake at night. If you feel sleepy during the day, get up, take a walk and get busy to keep from sleeping. Stretching is a good way to increase blood flow to the brain and keep you alert so that you don't sleep during the day. This will help you sleep better night.

A warm bath or a glass of milk in the evening can help your body relax and prepare for sleep. A cold bath will wake you up and keep you up for several hours. Also avoid eating too late before bed.

16. How would you describe this sentence?

    a. A recommendation

    b. An opinion

    c. A fact

    d. A diagnosis

17. Which of the following is an alternative title for this article?

    a. Exercise and a good night's sleep

    b. Benefits of a good night's sleep

    c. Tips for a good night's sleep

    d. Lack of sleep is a serious medical condition

18. Which of the following can not be inferred from this article?

    a. Biking is helpful for getting a good night's sleep

    b. Mental activity is helpful for getting a good night's sleep

    c. Eating bedtime snacks is not recommended

    d. Getting up at the same time is helpful for a good night's sleep

Questions 19 - 20 refer to the following passage.

Navy SEAL

The United States Navy's Sea, Air and Land Teams, commonly known as Navy SEALs, are the U.S. Navy's principal special operations force and a part of the Naval Special Warfare Command (NSWC) as well as the maritime component of the United States Special Operations Command (USSOCOM).

The unit's acronym ("SEAL") is comes from their capacity to operate at sea, in the air, and on land – but it is their ability to work underwater that separates SEALs from most other military units in the world. Navy SEALs are trained and have been deployed in a wide variety of missions, including direct action and special reconnaissance operations, unconventional warfare, foreign internal defense, hostage rescue, counter-terrorism and other missions. All SEALs are members of either the United States Navy or the United States Coast Guard.

In the early morning of 2 May 2011 local time, a team of 40 CIA-led Navy SEALs completed an operation to kill Osama bin Laden in Abbottabad, Pakistan about 35 miles (56 km) from Islamabad, the country's capital. The Navy SEALs were part of the Naval Special Warfare Development Group, previously called "Team 6". President Barack Obama later confirmed the death of bin Laden. The unprecedented media coverage raised the public profile of the SEAL community, particularly the counter-terrorism specialists commonly known as SEAL Team 6.

18. Are Navy Seals part of USSOCOM?

    a. Yes.

    b. No.

    c. Only for special operations.

    d. No, they are part of the US Navy.

20. What separates Navy SEALs from other military units?

    a. Belonging to NSWC.

    b. Direct action and special reconnaissance operations.

    c. Working underwater.

    d. Working for other military units in the world.

Mathematics

1. A map uses a scale of 1:100,000. How much distance on the ground is 3 inches on the map if the scale is in inches?

    a. 13 inches

    b. 300,000 inches

    c. 30,000 inches

    d. 333.999 inches

2. Divide 9.60 by 3.2.

    a. 2.50

    b. 3

    c. 2.3

    d. 6.4

3. Subtract 456,890 from 465,890.

    a. 9,000

    b. 7,000

    c. 8,970

    d. 8,500

4. Estimate 46,227 + 101,032.

    a. 14,700

    b. 147,000

    c. 14,700,000

    d. 104,700

5. Find the square of 25/9

    a. 5/3

    b. 3/5

    c. 7 58/81

    d. 15/2

6. Which one of the following is less than a third?

    a. 84/231

    b. 6/35

    c. 3/22

    d. b and c

7. Which of the following numbers is the largest?

    a. 1

    b. $\sqrt{2}$

    c. 3/2

    d. 4/3

8. 15/16 x 8/9 =

    a. 5/6

    b. 16/37

    c. 2/11

    d. 5/7

9. Driver B drove his car 20 km/h faster than the driver A, and driver B travelled 480 km 2 hours before driver A. What was the speed of driver A?

    a. 70

    b. 80

    c. 60

    d. 90

10. If a train travels at 72 kilometers per hour, how far will it travel in 12 seconds?

    a. 200 meters

    b. 220 meters

    c. 240 meters

    d. 260 meters

11. Tony bought 15 dozen eggs for $80. 16 eggs were broken during loading and unloading. He sold the remaining eggs for $0.54 each. What is his percent profit?

    a. 11%

    b. 11.2%

    c. 11.5%

    d. 12%

12. In a class of 83 students, 72 are present. What percent of students are absent?

    a. 12%

    b. 13%

    c. 14%

    d. 15%

13. In a local election at polling station A, 945 voters cast their vote out of 1270 registered voters. At polling station B, 860 cast their vote out of 1050 registered voters and at station C, 1210 cast their vote out of 1440 registered voters. What was the total turnout including all three polling stations?

 a. 70%

 b. 74%

 c. 76%

 d. 80%

14. Estimate 5205 ÷ 25

 a. 108

 b. 308

 c. 208

 d. 408

15. 7/15 – 3/10 =

 a. 1/6

 b. 4/5

 c. 1/7

 d. 1 1/3

16. Susan wants to buy a leather jacket that costs $545.00 and is on sale for 10% off. What is the approximate cost?

 a. $525

 b. $450

 c. $475

 d. $500

17. 11/20 ÷ 9/20 =

    a. 99/20

    b. 4 19/20

    c. 1 2/9

    d. 1 1/9

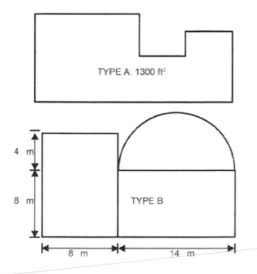

18. The price of houses in a certain subdivision is based on the total area. Susan is watching her budget and wants to choose the house with the lowest area. Which house type, A (1300 ft²) or B, should she choose if she would like the house with the lowest price?
(1cm² = 4.0ft² & π = 22/7)

    a. Type B is smaller 140 ft²

    b. Type A is smaller

    c. Type B is smaller at 855 ft²

    d. Type B is larger

19. Estimate 2009 x 108.

    a. 110,000

    b. 2,0000

    c. 21,000

    d. 210,000

20. Simplify 0.12 + 1 2/5 – 1 3/5

    a. 1 1/25

    b. 1 3/25

    c. 1 2/5

    d. 2 3/5

Algebra

21. Using the quadratic formula, solve the quadratic equation: $0.9x^2 + 1.8x - 2.7 = 0$

    a. 1 and 3

    b. -3 and 1

    c. -3 and -1

    d. -1 and 3

22. Subtract polynomials $4x^3 - 2x^2 - 10$ and $5x^3 + x^2 + x + 5$.

    a. $-x^3 - 3x^2 - x - 15$

    b. $9x^3 - 3x^2 - x - 15$

    c. $-x^3 - x^2 + x - 5$

    d. $9x^3 - x^2 + x + 5$

23. Find x and y from the following system of equations:

$(4x + 5y)/3 = ((x - 3y)/2) + 4$
$(3x + y)/2 = ((2x + 7y)/3) -1$

    a. (1, 3)

    b. (2, 1)

    c. (1, 1)

    d. (0, 1)

24. Using the factoring method, solve the quadratic equation: $x^2 + 12x - 13 = 0$

    a. -13 and 1

    b. -13 and -1

    c. 1 and 13

    d. -1 and 13

25. Using the quadratic formula, solve the quadratic equation:

$$\frac{x+2}{x-2} + \frac{x-2}{x+2} = 0$$

    a. It has infinite numbers of solutions

    b. 0 and 1

    c. It has no solutions

    d. 0

26. Turn the following expression into a simple polynomial:

$5(3x^2 - 2) - x^2(2 - 3x)$

    a. $3x^3 + 17x^2 - 10$

    b. $3x^3 + 13x^2 + 10$

    c. $-3x^3 - 13x^2 - 10$

    d. $3x^3 + 13x^2 - 10$

27. Solve $(x^3 + 2)(x^2 - x) - x^5$.

    a. $2x^5 - x^4 + 2x^2 - 2x$

    b. $-x^4 + 2x^2 - 2x$

    c. $-x^4 - 2x^2 - 2x$

    d. $-x^4 + 2x^2 + 2x$

28. $9ab^2 + 8ab^2 =$

    a. ab^2

    b. $17ab^2$

    c. 17

    d. $17a^2b^2$

29. Factor the polynomial $x^2 - 7x - 30$.

    a. $(x + 15)(x - 2)$

    b. $(x + 10)(x - 3)$

    c. $(x - 10)(x + 3)$

    d. $(x - 15)(x + 2)$

30. If a and b are real numbers, solve the following equation: $(a + 2)x - b = -2 + (a + b)x$

    a. -1

    b. 0

    c. 1

    d. 2

31. If $A = -2x^4 + x^2 - 3x$, $B = x^4 - x^3 + 5$ and $C = x^4 + 2x^3 + 4x + 5$, find $A + B - C$.

    a. $x^3 + x^2 + x + 10$

    b. $-3x^3 + x^2 - 7x + 10$

    c. $-2x^4 - 3x^3 + x^2 - 7x$

    d. $-3x^4 + x^3 + x^2 - 7x$

32. $(4Y^3 - 2Y^2) + (7Y^2 + 3y - y) =$

    a. $4y^3 + 9y^2 + 4y$

    b. $5y^3 + 5y^2 + 3y$

    c. $4y^3 + 7y^2 + 2y$

    d. $4y^3 + 5y^2 + 2y$

33. Turn the following expression into a simple polynomial: $1 - x(1 - x(1 - x))$

    a. $x^3 + x^2 - x + 1$

    b. $-x^3 - x^2 + x + 1$

    c. $-x^3 + x^2 - x + 1$

    d. $x^3 + x^2 - x - 1$

34. $7(2y + 8) + 1 - 4(y + 5) =$

    a. $10y + 36$

    b. $10y + 77$

    c. $18y + 37$

    d. $10y + 37$

35. Richard gives 's' amount of salary to each of his 'n' employees weekly. If he has 'x' amount of money then how many days he can employ these 'n' employees.

    a. $sx/7n$

    b. $7x/nx$

    c. $nx/7s$

    d. $7x/ns$

36. Factor the polynomial $x^2 - 3x - 4.$

    a. $(x + 1)(x - 4)$

    b. $(x - 1)(x + 4)$

    c. $(x - 1)(x - 4)$

    d. $(x + 1)(x + 4)$

37. Solve the inequality:

2x + 1/2x - 1 < 1

    a. $(-2, +\infty)$
    b. $(1, +\infty)$
    c. $(-\infty, -2)$
    d. $(-\infty, 1/2)$

38. Using the quadratic formula, solve the quadratic equation:

$(a^2 - b^2)x^2 + 2ax + 1 = 0$

    a. $a/(a + b)$ and $b/(a + b)$
    b. $1/(a + b)$ and $a/(a + b)$
    c. $a/(a + b)$ and $a/(a - b)$
    d. $-1/(a + b)$ and $1/(a - b)$

39. Turn the following expression into a simple polynomial: (a + b) (x + y) + (a - b) (x - y) - (ax + by)

    a. ax + by
    b. ax - by
    c. $ax^2 + by^2$
    d. $ax^2 - by^2$

40. Given polynomials A = $4x^5 - 2x^2 + 3x - 2$ and B = $-3x^4 - 5x^2 - 4x + 5$, find A + B.

    a. $x^5 - 3x^2 - x - 3$
    b. $4x^5 - 3x^4 + 7x^2 + x + 3$
    c. $4x^5 - 3x^4 - 7x^2 - x + 3$
    d. $4x^5 - 3x^4 - 7x^2 - x - 7$

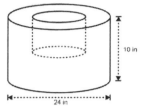

41. What is the volume of the above solid made by a hollow cylinder with half in size of the larger cylinder?

     a. $1440 \, \pi \, in^3$

     b. $1260 \, \pi \, in^3$

     c. $1040 \, \pi \, in^3$

     d. $960 \, \pi \, in^3$

42. Find x if $\log_{1/2} x = 4$.

     a. 16

     b. 8

     c. 1/8

     d. 1/16

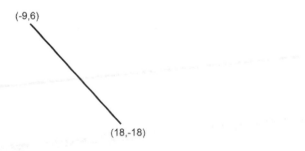

43. What is the slope of the line above?

     a. -8/9

     b. 9/8

     c. -9/8

     d. 8/9

44. If the sequence {a_n} is defined by a_{n+1} = 1- a_n and a_2 = 6, find a_4.

    a. 2

    b. 1

    c. 6

    d. -1

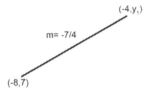

$(-4,y_1)$

m= -7/4

$(-8,7)$

45. With the data given above, what is the value of y_1?

    a. 0

    b. -7

    c. 7

    d. 8

46. The area of a rectangle is 20 cm². If one side increases by 1 cm and other by 2 cm, the area of the new rectangle is 35 cm². Find the sides of the original rectangle.

    a. (4,8)

    b. (4,5)

    c. (2.5,8)

    d. b and c

47. Solve $\log_{10} 10,000$ = x.

    a. 2

    b. 4

    c. 3

    d. 6

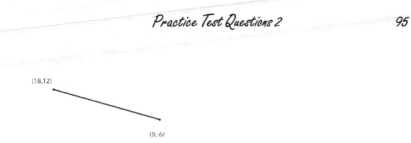

(18,12)

(9,-6)

48. What is the distance between the two points?

    a. ≈19

    b. 20

    c. ≈21

    d. ≈20

49. If in the right triangle, a is 12 and sinα=12/13, find cosα.

    a. -5/13

    b. -1/13

    c. 1/13

    d. 5/13

50. Find the solution for the following linear equation: 1/4 x - 2 = 5/6

    a. 0.2

    b. 0.4

    c. 0.6

    d. 0.8

(-1,2)

(-4,-4)

51. What is the slope of the line above?

    a. 1

    b. 2

    c. 3

    d. -2

52. How much water can be stored in a cylindrical container 5 meters in diameter and 12 meters high?

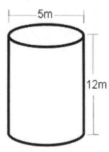

    a. 235.65 m³

    b. 223.65 m³

    c. 240.65 m³

    d. 252.65 m³

53. If members of the sequence {an} are represented by $a_{n+1} = -a_{n-1}$ and $a_2 = 3$ and, find $a_3 + a_4$.

    a. 2

    b. 3

    c. 0

    d. -2

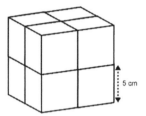

5 cm

54. What is the volume of the figure above?

    a. 125 cm³

    b. 875 cm³

    c. 1000 cm³

    d. 500 cm³

55. Solve

$x \sqrt{5} - y = \sqrt{5}$
$x - y \sqrt{5} = 5$

    a. $(0, -\sqrt{5})$

    b. $(0, \sqrt{5})$

    c. $(-\sqrt{5}, 0)$

    d. $(\sqrt{5}, 0)$

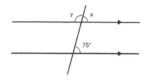

56. What is the value of the angle y?

    a. 25°

    b. 15°

    c. 30°

    d. 105°

57. Using the right triangle's legs, calculate (sinα + cosβ)/(tgα + ctgβ).

    a. a/b

    b. b/c

    c. b/a

    d. a/c

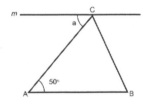

58. If the line *m* is parallel to the side AB of △ABC, what is angle *a*?

    a. 130°

    b. 25°

    c. 65°

    d. 50°

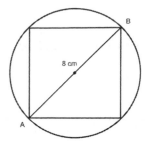

59. What is area of the circle?

    a. 4 π cm²

    b. 12 π cm²

    c. 10 π cm²

    d. 16 π cm²

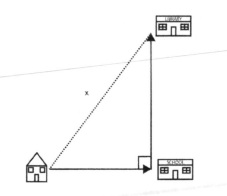

60. Every day starting from his home, Peter travels due east to school. After school, he travels due north to the library. This way Peter travels 25 kilometers. What is the distance between Peter's home and the library?

    a. 15 km

    b. 10 km

    c. 5 km

    d. 12 ½ km

Writing Skills

Directions: Select the best version of the underlined portion of the sentence

1. <u>Who</u> won first place in the Western Division?

    a. Whom won first place in the Western Division?

    b. Which won first place in the Western Division?

    c. What won first place in the Western Division?

    d. No change is necessary?

2. There are now several ways to listen to music, including radio, CDs, and Mp3 files <u>which</u> you can download onto an MP3 player.

    a. There are now several ways to listen to music, including radio, CDs, and Mp3 files on which you can download onto an MP3 player.

    b. There are now several ways to listen to music, including radio, CDs, and Mp3 files who you can download onto an MP3 player.

    c. There are now several ways to listen to music, including radio, CDs, and Mp3 files whom you can download onto an MP3 player.

    d. No change is necessary.

3. As the tallest monument in the United States, the St. Louis Arch <u>was rose to an impressive 630 feet</u>.

    a. As the tallest monument in the United States, the St. Louis Arch has rose to an impressive 630 feet.

    b. As the tallest monument in the United States, the St. Louis Arch is risen to an impressive 630 feet.

    c. As the tallest monument in the United States, the St. Louis Arch rises to an impressive 630 feet.

d. No change is necessary.

4. The tired, old woman should <u>lain</u> on the sofa.

a. The tired, old woman should lie on the sofa.

b. The tired, old woman should lays on the sofa.

c. The tired, old woman should laid on the sofa.

d. No changes are necessary.

5. Did the students understand that Thanksgiving always <u>fallen</u> on the fourth Thursday in November?

a No change is necessary.

b. Did the students understand that Thanksgiving always falling on the fourth Thursday in November.

c. Did the students understand that Thanksgiving always has fell on the fourth Thursday in November.

d. Did the students understand that Thanksgiving always falls on the fourth Thursday in November.

6. Collecting stamps, <u>build models</u>, and listening to shortwave radio were Rick's main hobbies.

a. Collecting stamps, building models, and listening to shortwave radio were Rick's main hobbies.

b. Collecting stamps, to build models, and listening to shortwave radio were Rick's main hobbies.

c. Collecting stamps, having built models, and listening to shortwave radio were Rick's main hobbies.

d. No change is necessary.

7. This morning, <u>after the kids will leave for school</u> and before the sun came up, my mother makes herself a cup of cocoa.

> a. This morning, after the kids had left for school and before the sun came up, my mother makes herself a cup of cocoa.

> b. This morning, after the kids leave for school and before the sun came up, my mother makes herself a cup of cocoa.

> c. This morning, after the kids have left for school and before the sun came up, my mother makes herself a cup of cocoa.

> d. No change is necessary.

8. Elaine promised to bring the camera <u>to me</u> at the mall yesterday.

> a. Elaine promised to bring the camera by me at the mall yesterday.

> b. Elaine promised to bring the camera with me at the mall yesterday.

> c. Elaine promised to bring the camera at me at the mall yesterday.

> d. No changes are necessary.

9. Last night, he <u>laid</u> the sleeping bag down beside my mattress.

> a. Last night, he lay the sleeping bag down beside my mattress.

> b. Last night, he lain

> c. Last night, he has laid

> d. No change is necessary.

10. I would have bought the shirt for you <u>if I know</u> you liked it.

> a. I would have bought the shirt for you if I had known you liked it.
>
> b. I would have bought the shirt for you if I have known you liked it.
>
> c. I would have bought the shirt for you if I would know you liked it.
>
> d. No change is necessary.

11. George wrecked John's <u>car; that</u> was the end of their friendship.

> a. George wrecked John's car that was the end of their friendship.
>
> b. George wrecked John's car. that was the end of their friendship.
>
> c. The sentence is correct.
>
> d. None of the choices are correct.

12. The dress was not Gina's <u>favorite, however,</u> she wore it to the dance.

> a. The dress was not Gina's favorite; however, she wore it to the dance.
> b. None of the choices are correct.
> c. The dress was not Gina's favorite, however; she wore it to the dance.
> d. The dress was not Gina's favorite however, she wore it to the dance.

13. Chris showed his dedication to golf in many <u>ways;</u> <u>for</u> example, he watched all of the tournaments on television.

a. Chris showed his dedication to golf in many ways, for example, he watched all of the tournaments on television.

b. The sentence is correct.

c. Chris showed his dedication to golf in many ways, for example; he watched all of the tournaments on television.

d. Chris showed his dedication to golf in many ways for example he watched all of the tournaments on television.

14. Choose the sentence with the correct grammar.

a. If Joe had told me the truth, I wouldn't have been so angry.
b. If Joe would have told me the truth, I wouldn't have been so angry.
c. I wouldn't have been so angry if Joe would have told the truth.
d. If Joe would have telled me the truth, I wouldn't have been so angry.

15. Until you <u>take</u> the overdue books to the library, you can't <u>take</u> any new ones home.

a. Until you take the overdue books to the library, you can't take any new ones home
b. Until you take the overdue books to the library, you can't bring any new ones home.
c. Until you bring the overdue books to the library, you can't take any new ones home.
d. None of the choices are correct.

16. If they had <u>gone</u> to the party, he would have <u>gone</u> too.

    a. The sentence is correct.

    b. If they had went to the party, he would have gone too.

    c. If they had gone to the party, he would have went too.

    d. If they had went to the party, he would have went too.

17. His doctor suggested that he eat <u>fewer</u> snacks and do <u>fewer</u> lounging on the couch.

    a. His doctor suggested that he eat less snacks and do fewer lounging on the couch.

    b. His doctor suggested that he eat fewer snacks and do less lounging on the couch.

    c. His doctor suggested that he eat less snacks and do less lounging on the couch.

    d. None of the choices are correct.

18. I can never remember how to use those two common words, "sell," meaning to trade a product for money, or <u>"to sale,"</u> meaning an event where products are traded for less money than usual.

    a. sale-

    b. "sale,"

    c. "sale

    d. None of the above are correct.

19. His father is <u>poet and novelist.</u>

    a. a poet and novelist

    b. a poet and a novelist

    c. either of the above

    d. none of the above

20. The class just finished reading , <u>Leinengen versus the Ants</u> a short story by Carl Stephenson about a plantation owner's battle with army ants.

    a. -"Leinengen versus the Ants",

    b. Leinengen versus the Ants,

    c. "Leinengen versus the Ants,"

    d. None of the above

21. My best friend said, "<u>Always Count your Change</u>."

    a. My best friend said, "always count your change."

    b. The sentence is correct.

    c. My best friend said, "Always count your change."

    d. None of the choices are correct.

22. He told him to <u>raised</u> it up.

    a. He told him to rise it up

    b. He told him to raise it up

    c. Either of the above

    d. None of the above

23. I shall arrive early and <u>have</u> breakfast with you.

    a. I shall arrive early and I will have breakfast with you

    b. I shall arrive early and I would have breakfast with you

    c. The sentence is correct.

    d. None of the above

24. The gold coins with the diamonds <u>are</u> to be seized.

    a. The gold coins with the diamonds is to be seized

    b. The sentence is correct.

    c. None of the above

25. The trousers is to be delivered today.

    a The trousers are to be delivered today

    b. The sentence is correct

    c. Both of the above

26. She was nodding her head, her hips were swaying.

    a. She was nodding her head, her hips are swaying.

    b. She was nodding her head, her hips is swaying.

    c. The sentence is correct.

    d. None of the above

27. The sad news are delivered this morning.

    a. The sad news were delivered this morning

    b. The sentence is correct.

    c. The sad news was delivered this morning

    d. None of the above

28. Mathematics were my best subject in school.

    a. The sentence is correct

    b. Mathematics are my best subject in school

    c. Mathematics was my best subject in school

    d. None of the above

29. 15 minutes <u>is</u> all the time you have to complete the test.

    a. The sentence is correct.

    b. 15 minutes are all the time you have to complete the test.

    c. Both of the above.

    d. None of the above.

30. Everyone <u>have</u> to wear a black tie.

    a. Everyone are to wear a black tie.

    b. The sentence is correct.

    c. Everyone has to wear a black tie.

    d. None of the above.

Answer Key

Reading Comprehension

1. B
We can infer an important part of the respiratory system
are the lungs. From the passage, "Molecules of oxygen and
carbon dioxide are passively exchanged, by diffusion, between the gaseous external environment and the blood. This
exchange process occurs in the alveolar region of the lungs."
Therefore, one of the primary functions for the respiratory
system is the exchange of oxygen and carbon dioxide, and
this process occurs in the lungs. We can therefore infer that
the lungs are an important part of the respiratory system.

2. C
The process by which molecules of oxygen and carbon dioxide are passively exchanged is diffusion.
This is a definition type question. Scan the passage for references to "oxygen," "carbon dioxide," or "exchanged."

3. A
The organ that plays an important role in gas exchange in
amphibians is the skin.
Scan the passage for references to "amphibians," and find
the answer.

4. A
The three physiological zones of the respiratory system are
Conducting, transitional, respiratory zones.

5. A
We can infer that, an electrical discharge in the clouds
causes lightning.

The passage tells us that, "Lightning occurs when static
electricity inside clouds builds up and causes an electrical
charge,"

6. C
Being struck by lightning means, a ninety percent chance of surviving the strike.

From the passage, "statistics show that 90% of victims survive a lightning blast."

7. A
We know that lightning is static electricity from the third sentence in the passage. We also know that static electricity is caused by water droplets colliding with ice crystals. Therefore, Lightning is caused by water droplets colliding with ice crystals.

8. A
Low blood sugar occurs both in diabetics and healthy adults.

9. B
None of the statements are the author's opinion.

10. A
The author's purpose is the inform.

11. A
The only statement that is not a detail is, "A doctor can diagnosis this medical condition by asking the patient questions and testing."

12. B
This passage describes the different categories for traditional stories. The other options are facts from the passage, not the main idea of the passage. The main idea of a passage will always be the most general statement. For example, Option A, Myths, fables, and folktales are not the same thing, and each describes a specific type of story. This is a true statement from the passage, but not the main idea of the passage, since the passage also talks about how some cultures may classify a story as a myth and others as a folktale. The statement, from Option B, Traditional stories can be categorized in different ways by different people, is a more general statement that describes the passage.

Practice Test Questions 2   111

13. B

Option B is the best choice, categories that group traditional stories according to certain characteristics.

Options A and C are false and can be eliminated right away. Option D is designed to confuse. Option D may be true, but it is not mentioned in the passage.

14. D

The best answer is D, traditional stories themselves are a part of the larger category of folklore, which may also include costumes, gestures, and music.

All of the other options are false. Traditional stories are part of the larger category of Folklore, which includes other things, not the other way around.

15. A

The sentence is a recommendation.

16. C

Tips for a good night's sleep is the best alternative title for this article.

17. B

Mental activity is helpful for a good night's sleep is can not be inferred from this article.

18. C

This question tests the reader's vocabulary and contextualization skills. A may or may not be true, but focuses on the wrong function of the word "give" and ignores the rest of the sentence, which is more relevant to what the passage is discussing. B and D may also be selected if the reader depends too literally on the word "give", failing to grasp the more abstract function of the word that is the focus of answer C, which also properly acknowledges the entirety of the passage and its meaning.

19. A

Navy Seals are the maritime component of the United States Special Operations Command (USSOCOM).

20. C
Working underwater separates SEALs from other military units. This is taken directly from the passage.

Mathematics

1. B
1 inch on map = 100,000 inches on ground. So 3 inches on map = 3 x 100,000 = 300,000 inches on ground.

2. B
9.60/3.2 = 3

3. A
465,890 - 456,890 = 9,000.

4. B
46,227 + 101,032 is approximately 147,000. The exact answer is 147,259.

5. C
$(25/9)^2 = 625/81$

6. D
84/231 = 12/33 > 1/3
6/35 = 1/5 < 1/3
3/22 = 1/7 < 1/3

7. B
$\sqrt{2}$ is the largest number.
Here are the choices:

  a. 1

  b. $\sqrt{2}$ = 1.414

  c. 3/22 = .1563

  d. 4/3 = 1.33

8. A
First cancel out 15/16 x 8/9 to get 5/2 x 1/3, then multiply numerators and denominators to get 5/6.

9. B

$V_b = V_a - 20$
$S = 480$
$t_a + 2 = t_b$
$S = V_a t_a$
$t_a = S/V_a$

$S = V_b t_b$
$480 = (V_a - 20)(t_a + 2)$
$480 = (V_a - 20)(480/V_a + 2)$
$480 = 480 + 2V_a - 2 - 480/V_a - 40$
$2V_a^2 - 40V_a - 9600 = 0$
$V_a^2 - 20V_a - 4800 = 0$

$V_{a1,2} = 20 \pm \sqrt{400 + 4 - 4800} / 2$
$V_{a1,2} = 20 \pm 140 / 2$

$V_a = 80$

10. C

1 hour is equal to 3600 seconds and 1 kilometer is equal to 1000 meters. So a train covers 72,000 meters in 36,000 seconds.
Distance covered in 12 seconds = 12 × 72,000/3,600 = 240 meters.

11. A

Remaining number of eggs that Tony sold = 12×15 – 16 = 164. Total amount for selling 164 eggs = 164×0.54 = $89.56. Percentage profit = (88.56 – 80) × 100/80 = 10.7% The answer is required with 2 significant digits, round off to 11%.

12. B

Absent students = 83 – 72 = 11
Percent of absent students =   11/83 X 100 = 13.25
Reducing up to two significant digits = 13%.

13. D

Total votes cast = 945 + 860 + 1210 = 3015
Total registered voters at all 3 polling stations =
1270 + 1050 + 1440 = 3760
Turnout = 3015/3760 X 100 = 80%

14. C

The approximate answer to $5205 \div 25$ is 208. The exact answer is 208.2.

15. A

A common denominator is needed, a number which both 15 and 10 will divide into. So $14-9/30 = 5/30 = 1/6$

16. D

The jacket costs $545.00 so we can round up to $550. 10% of $550 is 55. We can round down to $50, which is easier to work with. $550 - $50 is $500. The jacket will cost about $500.

17. C

$11/20 \times 20/9 = 11/1 \times 1/9 = 11/9 = 1\,2/9$

18. C

Area of Type B $= [(12 \times 8) + (14 \times 8) + (1/2 \times 22/7 \times 7^2)]$

$96 + 112 + 77$

285 m^2

Converting to feet $= 3 \times 285 \text{ ft}^2$

Area of Type B $= 855 \text{ ft}^2$

19. D

2009×108 is approximately 210,000. The exact answer is 216,972.

20. B

$0.12 + 2/5 + 3/5$, Convert decimal to fraction to get $3/25 + 2/5 + 3/5$, $= (3 + 10 + 15)/25$, $= 28/25 = 1\,3/25$

21. B

$0.9x^2 + 1.8x - 2.7 = 0 \;\; * \; 10$

$9x^2 + 18x - 27 = 0 \div 9$
$x^2 + 2x - 3 = 0$

$x_{1,2} = -2 \pm \sqrt{2^2} - 4 * (-3)/2$
$x_{1,2} = -2 \pm \sqrt{4} + 12/2$
$x_{1,2} = -2 \pm \sqrt{16}/2$

$x_{1,2} = -2 \pm 4$
$x_1 = -2 + 4/2 = 1$
$x_2 = -2 - 4/2 = -3$

22. A
$(4x^3 - 2x^2 - 10) - (5x^3 + x^2 + x + 5)$
$4x^3 - 2x^2 - 10 - 5x^3 - x^2 - x - 5$
$-x^3 - 3x^2 - x - 15$

23. C
Divide both equations by 6, for,

$2(4x + 5y) = 3(x - 3y) + 24$
$3(3x + 7) = 2(2x + 7y) - 6$

$8x + 10y = 3x - 9y + 24$
$9x + 3y = 4x + 14y = 6$

$8x + 10y = 3x - 9y + 24$
$9x + 3y = 4x + 14y - 6$

$5x + 19y = 24$
$5x = 11y = -6$

$5x + 19y - (5x - 11y) = 24 - (-6)$
$5x + 19y - 5x + 11y = 24 + 6$

$30y = 30$
y = 1

$5x + 19y = 24$

$5x + 19 = 24$

$5x = 24 - 19 = 5$

x = 1

24. A
-13 and 1
$x^2 + 12x - 13$
$x^2 + 13x - x - 13 = 0$
$x(x + 13) - (x + 13) = 0$
$(x + 13)(x - 1) = 0$
$X = -13 \quad X = 1$

25. C
This equation has no solution.

$x^2 + 4x + 4 + x^2 - 4x + 4 / (x - 2)(x + 2) = 0$
$2x^2 + 8 / (x - 2)(x + 2) = 0 \Rightarrow 2x^2 + 8 = 0$
$x^2 + 4 = 0$
$x_{1,2} = 0 \pm \sqrt{-4 * 4} / 2$
$x_{1,2} = 0 \pm \sqrt{-16} / 2$
Solution for the square root of -16 is not a real number, so this equation has no solution.

26. D
$3x^3 + 13x^2 - 10$
$5(3x^2 - 2) - x^2(2 - 3x)$
$15x^2 - 10 - 2x^2 + 3x^3$
$3x^3 + 13x^2 - 10$

27. B
$-x^4 + 2x^2 - 2x$
$(x^3 + 2) (x^2 - x) - x^5$
$x^5 - x^4 + 2x^2 - 2x - x^5$
$-x^4 + 2x^2 - 2x$

28. B
$ab^2 (9 + 8) = 17ab^2$

29. C
$x^2 - 7x - 30 = x * x - 10x + 3x - 3 * 10 = x(x - 10) + 3(x - 10) = (x - 10) (x + 3)$

30. A
$(a + 2)x - b = -2 + (a + b)x$
$ax + 2x - b = -2 + ax + bx$
$ax + 2x - ax - bx = -2 + b$
$2x - bx = -2 + b$
$(2 - b)x = -(2 - b)$
$x = -(2 - b) : (2 - b)$
$x = -1$

31. C
$-2x^4 - 3x^3 + x^2 - 7x$
$A + B - C = (-2x^4 + x^2 - 3x) + (x^4 - x^3 + 5) - (x^4 + 2x^3 + 4x + 5)$
$-2x^4 + x^2 - 3x + x^4 - x^3 + 5 - x^4 - 2x^3 - 4x - 5$
$-2x^4 - 3x^3 + x^2 - 7x$

32. D
Remove parenthesis
$4Y^3 - 2Y^2 + 7Y^2 + 3Y - Y =$
add and subtract like terms, $4Y^3 + 5Y^2 + 2Y$

33. C
$1 - x(1 - x(1 - x))$
$1 - x(1 - x + x^2)$
$1 - x + x^2 - x^3$
$-x^3 + x^2 - x + 1$

34. D
Open parenthesis, $(7 \times 2y + 7 \times 8) + 1 - (4 \times y - 20) =$
$14y + 56 + 1 - 4y - 20,$
Collect like terms $= 14y - 4y + 56 + 1 - 20 = 10y + 37$

35. D
He pays 'ns' amount to the employees for 7 days. The 'x' amount will be for '7x/ns' days.

36. A
$x^2 - 3x - 4 = x * x + x - 4x - 4 = x(x + 1) - 4(x + 1) = (x + 1)(x - 4)$

37. D
$(2x + 1 / 2x - 1) < 1$
$(2x + 1 / 2x - 1) - 1 < 0$
$(2x + 1 - 2x + 1 / 2x - 1) < 0$
$2 / 2x - 1 < 0$

2 is a positive number, so

$2x - 1 < 0$
$2x < 1$
$x < 1/2$

38. D

$-\dfrac{1}{a+b}$ and $-\dfrac{1}{a-b}$

$(a^2-b^2)x^2+2ax+1=0$

$x_{1,2}=\dfrac{-2a\pm\sqrt{(2a)^2-4(a^2-b^2)}}{2(a^2-b^2)}$

$x_{1,2}=\dfrac{-2a\pm\sqrt{4a^2-4a^2+4b^2}}{2(a^2-b^2)}$

$x_{1,2}=\dfrac{-2a\pm\sqrt{4b^2}}{2(a^2-b^2)}$

$x_{1,2}=\dfrac{-2a\pm2b}{2(a^2-b^2)}$

$x_{1,2}=\dfrac{-a\pm b}{a^2-b^2}=\dfrac{-a\pm b}{(a-b)(a+b)}$

$x_1=\dfrac{-a+b}{(a-b)(a+b)}=\dfrac{-(a-b)}{(a-b)(a+b)}=-\dfrac{1}{(a+b)}$

$x_2=\dfrac{-a-b}{(a-b)(a+b)}=\dfrac{-(a+b)}{(a-b)(a+b)}=-\dfrac{1}{(a-b)}$

39. A

$(a+b)(x+y)+(a-b)(x-y)-(ax+by)$
$= ax + ay + bx + by + ax - ay - bx + by - ax - by$
$ax + by$

40. C

$4x^5 - 3x^4 - 7x^2 - x + 3$
$A + B = (4x^5 - 2x^2 + 3x - 2) + (-3x^4 - 5x^2 - 4x + 5)=$
$4x^5 - 2x^2 + 3x - 2 - 3x^4 - 5x^2 - 4x + 5$
$4x^5 - 3x^4 - 7x^2 - x + 3$

41. B

Total Volume = Volume of large cylinder - Volume of small cylinder
Volume of cylinder = area of base x height
Volume= ($\pi\ 12^2$x 10) - ($\pi\ 6^2$x 5), 1440π - 180π
Volume= 1260π in^3

42. D

$\log_{1/2}x = 4$
$(1/2)^4 = x$
$x = 1/16$

43. A

Slope (m) = $\dfrac{\text{change in y}}{\text{change in x}}$
$(x_1, y_1)=(-9,6)$ & $(x_2, y_2)= (18,-18)$

Slope = $(-18 - 6)/[18-(-9)] = -24/27 = -8/9$

44. C
$a_{n+1} = 1 - a_n$
$a_2 = 6$
$a_3 = 1 - a_2 = 1 - 6 = -5$
$a_4 = 1 - a_3 = 1 - (-5) = 1 + 5 = 6$

45. A
$x_1, = -4$, $(x_2, y_2) = (-8,7)$ & slope $= -7/4$
$(7 - y_1)/[-8-(-4)] = -7/4$
$(7 - y_1)/-4 = -7/4$
$7 - y_1 = 7$
$y_1 = 0$

46. D
$ab = 20 \Rightarrow a = 20/b$
$(a + 1)(b + 2) = 35$

$(20/b + 1)(b + 2) = 35$
$20 + 40/b + b + 2 = 35$
$20b + 40 + b^2 = 33b$
$b^2 - 13b + 40 = 0$
$b_{1,2} = 13 \pm \sqrt{169 - 160} / 2$
$b_{1,2} = 13 \pm 3 / 2$
$b_1 = 8$
$b_2 = 5$
$a_1 = 20/b_1 = 20/8 = 2.5$
$a_2 = 20/b_2 = 20/5 = 4$

47. B
$\log_{10} 10,000 = x$
$10^x = 10,000$
$10^x = 10^4$
$x = 4$

48. D
Distance between 2 points $= [(x_2 - x_1)^2 + (y_2 - y_1)^2]^{1/2}$

Distance $= [(18 - 9)^2 + (12 + 6)^2]^{1/2}$
Distance $= [(9)^2 + (18)^2]^{1/2}$
Distance $= (81 + 324)^{1/2}$
Distance $= (405)^{1/2}$

Since $20^2 = 400$ & $21^2 = 441$, $19^2 = 361$ therefore the distance is approximately 20.

49. D
a = 12
sina = 12/13 = a/c
a/c = 12/13
12/c = 12/13
c = 13
$a^2 + b^2 = c^2$
$12^2 + b^2 = 13^2$
$b^2 = 169 - 144$
$b^2 = 25$
b = 5
cosa = b/c = 5/13

50. D
1/4x - 2 = 5/6
1 = 5 (4x - 2)/6
6 = 5(4x - 2)
6 = 20x - 10
-20x = -10 - -6
-20x = -16
x = -16/-20 = 0.8

51. B
Slope (m) = change in y / change in x

(x_1, y_1) = (-1, 2) & (x_2, y_2) = (-4, -4)
Slope = (-4 – 2)/[-4 - (-1)] = -6/-3
Slope = 2

52. B
The formula of the volume of cylinder is = $\prod r^2h$. Where $\prod$ is 3.142, r is radius of the cross sectional area, and h is the height. So the volume will be = $3.142 \times 2.5^2 \times 12 = 235.65$ m³.

53. C
$a_{n+1} = - a_{n-1}$
$a_2 = 3$
$a_3 = - a_2 = -3$
$a_4 = - a_3 = -(-3) = 3$

$a_3 + a_4 = -3 + 3 = 0$

54. C
Large cube is made up of 8 smaller cubes of 5 cm sides.
Volume = Volume of small cube x 8
Volume = (5 x 5 x 5) x 8, 125 x 8
Volume = 1000 cm^3

55. A
$(0, -\sqrt{5})$

$y = x\sqrt{5} - \sqrt{5}$
$x - (x\sqrt{5} - \sqrt{5})\ \sqrt{5} = 5$
$x - 5x + 5 = 5$
$-4x = 5 - 5$
$-4x = 0$

$y = x\sqrt{5} - \sqrt{5}$
$y = 0\sqrt{5} - \sqrt{5}$
$y = \sqrt{5}$

Remove the brackets, but change all signs in the third polynomial because of the minus sign. Now group the variables
by degrees.

56. D
Two parallel lines intersected by a third line with angles of
75°
x = 75° (corresponding angles)
x + y = 180° (supplementary angles)
y = 180° - 75°
y = 105°

57. B
$(\sin\alpha + \cos\beta)/(tg\alpha + ctg\beta) = (a/c + a/c)/(a/b + a/b) = (2a/c)/$
$(2a/b) = b/c$

58. D
Two parallel lines(m & side AB) intersected by side AC
a = 50° (interior angles).

59. D
Circle with given diameter and a square within the circle

Area of circle = $\pi \times r^2$
Area of circle = $\pi \times 4^2$
Area of circle = 16π cm^2

The actual cost will be 10% X 545 = \$54.50
545 − 54.50 = \$490.50

60. C
Pythagorean Theorem:
(Hypotenuse)^2 = (Perpendicular)^2 + (Base)^2
$h^2 = a^2 + b^2$

Given: $a^2 + b^2 = 25$
$h^2 = 25$
h = 5, so the distance from Peter's home to the library is 5 km.

Writing Skills

1. D
"Who" is correct because the question uses an active construction. "To whom was first place given?" is passive construction.

2. D
"Which" is correct, because the files are objects and not people.

3. C
The simple present tense, "rises," is correct.

4. A
"Lie" does not require a direct object, while "lay" does. The old woman might lie on the couch, which has no direct object, or she might lay the book down, which has the direct object, "the book."

5. D
The simple present tense, "falls," is correct because it is repeated action.

6. A
The present progressive, "building models," is correct in this sentence; it is required to match the other present progressive verbs.

7. C
Past Perfect tense describes a completed action in the past, before another action in the past.

8. D
The preposition "to" is the correct preposition to use with "bring."

9. D
"Laid" is the past tense.

10. A
This is a past unreal conditional sentence. It requires an 'if' clause and a result clause, and either clause can appear first. The 'if' clause uses the past perfect, while the result clause uses the past participle.

11. C
The semicolon links independent clauses. An independent clause can form a complete sentence by itself.

12. A
The semicolon links independent clauses with a conjunction (However).

13. B
The sentence is correct. The semicolon links independent clauses. An independent clause can form a complete sentence by itself.

14. A
The third conditional is used for talking about an unreal situation (that did not happen) in the past. For example, "If I had studied harder, [if clause] I would have passed the exam [main clause]. Which is the same as, "I failed the exam, because I didn't study hard enough."

15. C
Bring vs. Take. Usage depends on your location. Something coming your way is brought to you. Something going away is taken from you.

16. A
The sentence is correct. Went vs. Gone. Went is the simple past tense. Gone is used in the past perfect.

17. B
Fewer vs. Less. 'Fewer' is used with countables and 'less' is used with uncountables.

18. B
Here the word "sale" is used as a "word" and not as a word in the sentence, so quotation marks are used.

19. B
His father is a poet and a novelist. It is necessary to use 'a' twice in this sentence for the two distinct things.

20. C
Titles of short stories are enclosed in quotation marks, and commas always go inside quotation marks.

21. A
Quoted speech is not capitalized.

22. B
The verb raise ('to increase', 'to lift up.') can appear in three forms, raise, raised and raised.

23. C
The two verbs "shall" and "will" should not be used in the same sentence when referring to the same future.

24. B
When two subjects are linked with "with" or "as well," use the verb form that matches the first subject.

25. A
Use a plural verb for nouns like measles, tongs, trousers, riches, scissors etc.

26. C
A verb can fit any of the two subjects in a compound sentence as long as the verb form agrees with that subject.

27. C
Always use the singular verb form for nouns like politics, wages, mathematics, innings, news, advice, summons, furniture, information, poetry, machinery, vacation, scenery etc.

28. C
Always use the singular verb form for nouns like politics, wages, mathematics, innings, news, advice, summons, furniture, information, poetry, machinery, vacation, scenery etc.

29. A
Use a singular verb with a plural noun that refers to a specific amount or quantity that is considered as a whole (dozen, hundred score etc).

30. C
Use a singular verb with either, each, neither, everyone and many.

Conclusion

CONGRATULATIONS! You have made it this far because you have applied yourself diligently to practicing for the exam and no doubt improved your potential score considerably! Getting into a good school is a huge step in a journey that might be challenging at times but will be many times more rewarding and fulfilling. That is why being prepared is so important.

Good Luck!

FREE Ebook Version

Download a FREE Ebook version of the publication!

Suitable for tablets, iPad, iPhone, or any smart phone.

Go to http://tinyurl.com/o85pghd

Register for Free Updates and More Practice Test Questions

Register your purchase at www.test-preparation.ca/register. html for fast and convenient access to updates, errata, free test tips and more practice test questions.

COMPASS Strategy

Multiple Choice Strategies for Basic Math, Word Problems, English Grammar and Reading Comprehension

INCREASE YOUR SCORE!

Multiple Choice and Test Taking Strategies!

Over 150 Practice Questions

Published by Complete TEST Preparation Inc.

COMPASS is a trademark of ACT, INC. who are not involved in the production of this book and do not endorse this book.

Learn to increase your score using time-tested secrets for answering multiple choice questions!

This practice book has everything you need to know about answering multiple choice questions on a standardized test!

You will learn 12 strategies for answering multiple choice questions and then practice each strategy with over 45 reading comprehension multiple choice questions, with extensive commentary from exam experts!

Maybe you have read this kind of thing before, and maybe feel you don't need it, and you are not sure if you are going to buy this book.

Remember though, it only a few percentage points divide the PASS from the FAIL students.

Even if our multiple choice strategies increase your score by a few percentage points, isn't that worth it?

Go to

https://www.createspace.com/4600674

Super Study Session

Can't Concentrate?

Can't settle down to study?

Scientifically proven to increase learning, focus, memory and long term retention!

Do you ever find that you can't seem to settle down to study? Are you distracted easily?

Binaural beats are the answer! You can't settle down to study because your brain is at the wrong frequency. One way to think of this is the Super Study Session changes the dial on your brain and puts you in study mode and keeps you there for 1 hour.

Learn More at

www.test-preparation.ca/study-music.html

Endnotes

[1] Immune System. In *Wikipedia*. Retrieved November 12, 2010 from, en.wikipedia.org/wiki/Immune_system.
[2] White Blood Cell. In *Wikipedia*. Retrieved November 12, 2010 from en.wikipedia.org/wiki/White_blood_cell.
[3] Infectious disease. In *Wikipedia*. Retrieved November 12, 2010 from http://en.wikipedia.org/wiki/Infectious_disease.
[4] Thunderstorm. In *Wikipedia*. Retrieved November 12, 2010 from en.wikipedia.org/wiki/Thunderstorm.
[5] Meteorology. In *Wikipedia*. Retrieved November 12, 2010 from en.wikipedia.org/wiki/Outline_of_meteorology.
[6] Cloud. In *Wikipedia*. Retrieved November 12, 2010 from http://en.wikipedia.org/wiki/Clouds.
[7] U.S. Navy Seal. In *Wikipedia*. Retrieved November 12, 2010 from en.wikipedia.org/wiki/United_States_Navy_SEALs.
[8] Respiratory System. In *Wikipedia*. Retrieved November 12, 2010 from en.wikipedia.org/wiki/Respiratory_system.
[9] Mythology. In *Wikipedia*. Retrieved November 12, 2010 from en.wikipedia.org/wiki/Mythology.
[10] What is Free Range Chicken In *Answers.com*. Retrieved Feb 14, 2009, from http://wiki.answers.com/Q/What_is_free-range_chicken.
[11] Grizzly Bear. In *Wikipedia*. Retrieved Feb 14, 2009, from http://en.wikipedia.org/wiki/Grizzly_Bear.
[12] Grizzly Polar Bear Hybrid. In *Wikipedia*. Retrieved Feb 14, 2009, from http://en.wikipedia.org/wiki/Grizzly%E2%80%93polar_bear_hybrid.
[13] Peafowl. In *Wikipedia*. Retrieved Feb 14, 2009, from en.wikipedia.org/wiki/Peafowl.
[14] Smallpox. In *Wikipedia*. Retrieved Feb 14, 2009, from http://en.wikipedia.org/wiki/Smallpox.

[15] Venus. In *Wikipedia*. Retrieved Feb 14, 2009, from http://en.wikipedia.org/wiki/Venus.
[16] Ebola In Wikipedia. Retrieved Feb 14, 2009 from http://en.wikipedia.org/wiki/Ebola.

ion can be obtained at www.ICGtesting.com
A
50314

00001B/302/P